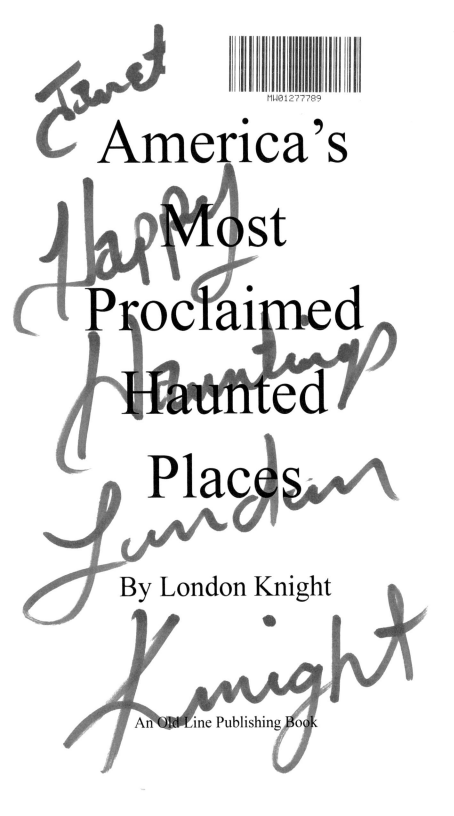

MW01277789

America's Most Proclaimed Haunted Places

By London Knight

An Old Line Publishing Book

Janet
Happy Haunting
London
Knight

Old Line Publishing, LLC
P.O. Box 624
Hampstead, MD 21074
Toll-Free Phone: 1-877-866-8820
Toll-Free Fax: 1-877-778-3756
Email: oldlinepublishing@comcast.net
Website: www.oldlinepublishingllc.com

America's Most Proclaimed Haunted Places

Dedications and Special Acknowledgements

I have traveled all around America in search of what truly lies on the other side of death. This is with great thanks to some amazing paranormal teams out there today. Special thanks goes to Jimmy Morris, founder of Texas Paranormal Research, the host of "Ghost Chatter" Radio Show, and the program director of PARA's X Radio.

"Ghost Chatter" airs every Wednesday at 8:00 p.m. eastern standard time. Anyone out there looking for a learned listening experience, this is a great show. The EVPs on some of the tracks on the DVD were sent from Jimmy and his team. Thanks Jimmy I could not have done this without you. I look forward to working with you on the next book. YOU ROCK!

To the listeners of "Ghost Chatter" Radio, you guys gave me some great ideas for places to investigate for the book.. Thank you.

To my husband Mike, who has been on this wild journey with me the whole way. And to my kids who have been in some of the scary places I've been while I was researching this book.

Special thanks to Wispers and SAPS for their contributions.

Thanks to Blaine "Big Sexy" Rohan, and Matt Hardigree, for the photographic and EVP support-you guys helped me to feel at home and your photographic and investigative talents are evident in this book.

A special thanks to TAPS for the outstanding contribution to the paranormal field, and with the work done in particular on the Northern State Ghost Hunters Episode.

And last but not least, to the owners of all the great places featured in this book. It is people like you who have reached out and helped make the paranormal community get that much closer to finding the answer of what truly lies out there.

America's Most Proclaimed Haunted Places

<u>Warning</u>

Please understand all of the places listed within the pages of this book require permission to visit or investigate. They are patrolled by the authorities and trespassers will be prosecuted. Many of the places within this book are very old. Some date as far back as the late 1800's and are very dangerous, as well as structurally unsound.

No one should ever go alone or without permission.

Many of the crime scene photos within this book may be too explicit and raw for some readers. Parental discretion and guidance is advised.

America's Most Proclaimed Haunted Places

Table of Contents

America's Most Proclaimed Haunted Places

Types of Paranormal Activity

Intelligent Hauntings

A haunting by a spirit which interacts with the living; an intelligent or interactive presence capable of communication or attempted communication with the living; a ghost or spirit that is aware of its state and able to communicate; type of haunting considered to be intelligent due to the fact that attempted communication with the living usually occurs.

Residual Hauntings

These haunting are said to be caused by a tremendous traumatic event that can release a substantial amount of energy into the atmosphere. This causes the atmosphere to imprint or record the event, much as a video or tape recording of the event.

The sprits are unaware of their surroundings or of the living within it. There is no interaction between them and the living. They are oftentimes associated with anniversaries and/or similar conditions.

These residual hauntings are often reported as being associated with quartz, crystal, and/or limestone and granite deposits within the geography of the haunted land.

Poltergeist Hauntings

These hauntings share many characteristics of an intelligent haunting. This is perhaps the most frightening type of haunting, as it is oftentimes the most active. It is often brought on by a teenager during stressful situations. This type of haunting is also often

America's Most Proclaimed Haunted Places

Common Paranormal Investigative Tools

EMF Detectors

EMF Detectors are better known as Electromagnetic Field Detectors. It is widely believed that Spirits are composed of Energy. The Spirit, in order to make contact with the living, needs to gather energy. Many believe this is what causes cold spots. EMF detectors are used by paranormal investigators to measure the Electromagnetic field at a given location. After taking a base reading, any fluctuation detected afterwards by an EMF detector, and in conjunction with a noise (or EVP) recording could indicate a paranormal presence or a Spirit.

K2 Detectors

The K2 is much like the standard EMF detector. Chris Fleming, a psychic medium from the show titled, *DEAD FAMOUS*, attempted to use the K2 in conjunction with what he picked up with his psychic abilities. He found the K2 accurate during his studies and used it on his TV show, thus bringing it to use in the paranormal world.

Ghost Box

It was speculated that Thomas Edison worked on a box to communicate with the dead using EVP theory, Electronic Voice Phenomena. EVP was discovered in the late 1950's and has become well known today within the paranormal world due to television shows featuring ghost investigators.

Simply stated, it is a communications device between the

associated with high levels of minerals and limestone within the ground or the surrounding area. Also common with these types of suspected hauntings are objects moving, stacking, and disembodied voices being heard.

<u>Demonic Hauntings</u>

This is indeed one that is very rare. Only a hand-full of paranormal investigators are trained to handle these. Rarely does your average paranormal investigator run across a demonic haunting or possession case.

Demons are entities never born to this earth and do not possess a mortal soul. Some classify a demon as pure negative energy. They are often accompanied by a foul odor, most often reported as resembling the smell of rotten flesh. A demon is able to take on any form of its choosing, from animal to human.

As I was writing this, I was having trouble defining a demonic force, so I called my friend and well-known demonologist, Loraine Warren. She put it in its simplest definition, and I quote, "It is that of an inhuman haunting."

<u>*Orbs*</u>

Some believe these are Spirits trying to manifest themselves. They can be captured in photographs and classified as light anomalies. But, they also could be reflections of flash on moisture in the air, bugs, and dust particles, just to name a few obvious explanations. Orbs are highly debated in paranormal circles. As for me, I do not hold much faith in orbs. There simply is just not enough evidence on them, as of yet.

realms of the living and the dead.

The Frank Box is what is known as a ghost box - the first of its kind. It is a device that produces random voltage to create raw audio from an AM tuner, where it is then amplified and fed into an echo chamber and recorded.

"A real time two way communication device" – The first of its kind accepted by most paranormal investigators.

~ CHAPTER ONE ~

~ The Amityville House~
Amityville, New York

Ronald lay awake in the darkness of the late night now surrounding him. It is only the voice that whispers within his own head keeping him from sleep.

"Wake up... You know what it is you must do... Kill them—all of them!" Ronald heard as he looked at the small clock on the nightstand beside his bed: three a.m. It is the voice that calls to him. A voice from one he cannot see. A voice within the darkness of the night that only grows louder as the minutes pass until the sound is deafening.

Ronald gets up and kneels beside his bed, reaching under it, he removes the shotgun. As he walks down the hall to where his parents lie unsuspecting, asleep in their bed, the voices call louder and louder, *"Kill them... Kill them all!"* Moving to the command of the voice, he stands over his parents' bed. The silence of the night is broken by the sound of the shots ringing out, loudly echoing from the house. Then four more follow. Soon, the silence returns once more, and the voice that haunted Ronald until now, speaks no more.

Until months later, when a family named Lutz moved in. As the days passed, the house seemed to come to life, calling out for blood once again. Speaking to George: *"They are not your family but that of demons. You know what you must do. Kill them! Send them back to hell! Before it is too late. Look at them. Look close within their eyes! They're not your family. You can see the evil within them. Kill them! Before it is too late."* Luckily, George and his family escaped the evil Ronald Defeo, Jr. was not able to.

The majority of us have either seen the movies or read the numerous books on the old English colonial house with the trademark, quarter–circle, bay window sitting at 112 Ocean Avenue in Amityville, New York; the very famous Amityville horror house—a house whose reputation precedes it. A house the owners claim "held within it the devil, himself." A house so evil it made a family flee from it, under the cover of the darkness of night. Yet, for most of us, we have not had the chance to see all the evidence surrounding the legend of the Amityville house or the murders which took place on the early morning of November 13, 1974. Could demonic forces really be so evil they would cause a man to brutally murder his whole family as they lay sleeping in their beds? Or was the story behind the house at 112 Ocean Avenue simply a fable made up by a cold-blooded killer, drugged up on LSD, in a failed attempt for an insanity plea?

In order to uncover the truth behind the Amityville house, and the murders that took place there, we must start at the beginning. We must start back at a time when Suffolk County, New York, belonged to the Shinnecock Indian Tribe. Back in the 1700s, they used the land in Amityville as their burial grounds. In the late 1700s, the Shinnecock Indians lost their land and the settlers moved in. In 1782 a family attempted to build a house on the land near to where the Amityville house sits today, but it seemed the land would not allow it.

During the construction of the house, the owners' oldest son came across a skull that had been unearthed, and he began to play football with it. That very day, the land seemed to change. The workers would get hurt or fall violently ill while on the land. Fires would even start out of nowhere. Soon, no one would work on the land and the construction on the house was put on hold. Months later, the owner finally found workers to finish building the house. But the day it was to be completed, the house burned to the ground. The owner, frustrated with what had been going on, sold the land.

As the years passed, the land went through many hands. Then in 1924 the land was sold to a woman named Eileen Fitzgerald, builder of the house sitting there today. After further investigation into the land deed, it is not clear if the land was given to her by family or if she bought it. In 1960, Eileen Fitzgerald sold the house to a family by the name of Rilet then, only five years later, it was sold to the Defeo's.

Ronald and Louise DeFeo bought the house for its convenience to the Buick dealership belonging to Louise's father, and that Ronald, Sr. ran. Ronald, Sr. felt the house in Long Island would be a better fit for their large family. It included himself, Louise, and their five children: Ronald, Jr., better known as Butch by friends and family, Dawn, Allison, Mark, and John. He would have been able to give his family the life he always wanted.

But, like most older kids, Butch did not take to leaving his friends and the only place he had known as home, the city of New York. It was at this time Butch got into heavy drugs. Mainly LSD and cocaine, this excessive drug use caused Ronald, Jr.'s temper to accelerate out of control. Ronald, Jr., at that time, also became fascinated with guns. There was even one occasion where, after an

17

argument with his father, Ronald, Jr. grabbed one of his shotguns, aimed at his father with the family looking on, and pulled the trigger. Whether the shotgun was loaded or simply failed to discharge, only Ronald, Jr. will ever know. To Ronald, Sr. and his wife Louise, their oldest son had spiraled out of control. He became an embarrassment to their family.

Butch would often hold all night parties and his constant use of drugs became too much for Ronald, Sr., especially when Dawn started following in her brother's footsteps. In response, Ronald, Sr. grew overbearing and controlling over his children; often disciplining them with a heavy hand.

This pushed Ronald, Jr. to become even more difficult and more withdrawn. In early November, with Butch's drug habit out of control, he often found himself broke from spending his money on his drug habit. Police records indicate that, only days before the murders, Ronald, Jr. staged a robbery as he was making the deposit from the Buick dealership. Ronald, Sr. reached his limit and had enough of his son's bad behavior. Taking matters into his own hands, he threatened to fire him and have him put in jail. The events that took place next would make headlines all across America and turn the quiet town of Amityville upside down for years to come.

On November 13, 1974, around three-fifteen a.m., Ronald "Butch" Defeo, Jr. would completely lose it all together. As Ronald and three of his friends sat partying, and the rest of his family slept, Ronald, Jr. made the fateful decision to get rid of the one thing he believed was holding him back from the life he wanted—his family. With his parents out of the way, and the money from both the Buick dealership and their life insurance money, Ronald thought he would finally be free.

As the house lay dark, Ronald, Jr., armed himself with a .35 caliber rifle. He moved through the darkness of the house to his parents' bedroom, followed by his sister, Dawn. He stood in the doorway of his parents' room watching them sleep. He then pointed the .35 caliber rifle at his father and pulled the trigger. Breaking the silence of the night itself, he then turned the rifle on his mother.

At this point, it is believed, Dawn and Ronald, Jr. struggled for the gun with Dawn the obvious loser of the struggle. According to the coroner's report, the gun powder on Dawn's nightgown was from the barrel of the gun. This is also consistent with the blood spatter pattern found at the foot of her parent's bed. Dawn's body was also moved at least twice throughout the course of the night. At what time and whether after the murders or the following morning, only Ronald, Jr. really knows. After killing his mother and father, Ronald, Jr. moved to the bedroom shared by his brothers, Mark and John. Once again, raising his rifle he shot them both. But it was Allison who would live out the nightmare of that night longest as she was the last of the Defeo's to have been murdered. Then the silence returned to the Defeo household. A permanent silence fell over the DeFeo household.

What happened next, by Ronald, Jr.'s own admission, was nothing short of the acts of a mad man with no conscience. Ronald got rid of the gun. Then he returned to the house and took a shower. This was in the very bathroom adjoining Allison's room, where she now lay dead by his hand. He then got ready and left for work at the dealership. Most believed that after work, Ronald returned home and arranged the bodies of his family to make it look like a robbery took place. This would be consistent with the photos of Dawn's body in the three separate parts of the house. Ronald, Jr. left the house and stopped by a local bar he visited on numerous occasions. Ronald would then return to the house with the men from the bar. One of which was Joey Yeswit, the man who made the 9-1-1 call from within the house.

Figure 1. Removal of the bodies from the Amityville house.

Transcript of the Actual 9-1-1-Phone Call

Operator: This is Suffolk County Police. May I help you?"

Man: "We have a shooting here. Uh, DeFeo."

Operator: "Sir, what is your name?"

Man: "Joey Yeswit."

Operator: "Can you spell that?"

Man: "Yeah. Y-E-S W I T."

Operator: "Y-E-S...

Man: "Y-E-S-W-I-T."

Operator: ". . . W-I-T. Your phone number?"

Man: "I don't even know if it's here. There's, uh, I don't have a phone number here."

Operator: "Okay, where you calling from?"

Man: "It's in Amityville. Call up the Amityville Police, and it's right off, uh... Ocean Avenue in Amityville."

Operator: "Austin?"

Man: "Ocean Avenue. What the ..."

Operator: "Ocean ... Avenue? Offa where?"

Man: "It's right off Merrick Road. Ocean Avenue."

Operator: "Merrick Road. What's ... what's the problem, Sir?"

Man: "It's a shooting!"

Operator: "There's a shooting. Anybody hurt?"

Man: "Hah?"

Operator: "Anybody hurt?"

Man: "Yeah, it's uh, uh— everybody's dead."

Operator: "Whattaya mean, everybody's dead?"

Man: "I don't know what happened. Kid come running in the bar.
He says everybody in the family was killed, and we came
down here."

Operator: "Hold on a second, Sir."

(Police Officer now takes over call)

Police Officer: "Hello."

Man: "Hello."

Police Officer: "What's your name?"

Man: "My name is Joe Yeswit."

Police Officer: "George Edwards?"

Man: "Joe Yeswit."

Police Officer: "How do you spell it?"

Man: "What? I just... How many times do I have to tell you? Y-E-S
-W-I-T."

Police Officer: "Where're you at?"

Man: "I'm on Ocean Avenue.

Police Officer: "What number?"

Man: "I don't have a number here. There's no number on the
phone."

Police Officer: "What number on the house?"

Man: "I don't even know that."

Police Officer: "Where're you at? Ocean Avenue and what?"

Man: "In Amityville. Call up the Amityville Police and have someone come down here. They know the family."

Police Officer: "Amityville."

Man: "Yeah, Amityville."

Police Officer: "Okay. Now, tell me what's wrong."

Man: "I don't know. Guy come running in the bar. Guy come running in the bar and said there—his mother and father are shot. We ran down to his house and everybody in the house is shot. I don't know how long, you know. So, uh..."

Police Officer: "Uh, what's the add... What's the address of the house?"

Man: "Uh, hold on. Let me go look up the number. All right. Hold on. One-twelve, Ocean Avenue, Amityville."

Police Officer: "Is that Amityville or North Amityville?"

Man: "Amityville. Right on... South of Merrick Road."

Police Officer: "Is it right in the village limits?"

Man: "It's in the village limits, yeah."

Police Officer: "Eh, okay, what's your phone number?"

Man: "I don't even have one. There's no number on the phone. "

Police Officer: "All right, where're you calling from? Public phone?"

Man: "No, I'm calling right from the house, because I don't see a number on the phone."

Police Officer: "You're at the house itself?"

Man: "Yeah."

Police Officer: "How many bodies are there?"

Man: "I think, uh, I don't know—uh, I think they said four."

Police Officer: "There's four?"

Man: "Yeah."
Police Officer: "All right, you stay right there at the house, and I'll call the Amityville Village P.D., and they'll come down."

Once the police arrived at the house, they found one of the most disturbing scenes Amityville has ever encountered. The police instantly went to work: taping off one of the largest crime scenes and most gruesome murders to hit Amityville. They were looking for a killer they believed to still be on the loose. It was not long before the inconsistencies in Ronald Jr.'s stories led the police straight to Ronald.

After their search of the property the police turned up the .35 caliber rifle in the creek, out by the boathouse. And it was with that evidence they arrested Ronald, Jr. and charged him with six counts of murder. He was incarcerated on November 14. On November 18th, Ronald, Jr. was examined by the Suffolk County jail psychiatrist and found competent to stand trial.

2343

animal was quiet.

Members of the jury, the People will prove that sometime after three a.m. on November 13th Ronald DeFeo pointed the death weapon at his father's back and fired it. It took Ronald DeFeo, Jr., two shots to kill his father. One of these entered his back and passed through his body, destroying his heart. And there is no definitive proof as to where precisely Ronald DeFeo, Sr., was at that point in time his son fired the first shot into his back. That bullet, you may infer, stopped inside of his body.

Testimony by the Deputy Chief Medical Examiner who examined this body as it was found laying face down in his bed, combined with his autopsy conducted later that night at the Medical Examiner's office in Hauppauge, will show that the trajectories of each bullet which entered his back were different. The difference in the angles of these bullets entering the body combined with certain other evidence in the case that you will learn of may cause you to conclude that this Defendant first shot his father after he had gotten up from his bed, and

24

2344

thereafter his body--the body of his father was
placed back into bed to be found later by police.

2345

her and plced the muzzle of his gun less than two
feet from her face. The proof will show that
Allison DeFeo had awakened and raised her head
toward the door where her murderer stood at the
moment of her death. He fired into her head, and
the bullet destroyed the girl's brain before it
passed through the opposite ear, through the
bedding, bouncing off the wall at the head of the
bed, coming to rest on the floor beneath it. Her
death, too, was instantaneous. And the position
of her body and death, as you will observe, sug-
gests that she died as she was awakening from her
sleep.

Ronald DeFeo then ejected the spent cartridge
into a spreading pool of his sister's blood and
turned toward the bedroom of his sleeping brothers
Mark and John just steps away on the same floor.
Each boy occupied a bed on opposite sides of the
bedroom, and they lay parallel to one another.
We will offer evidence that Mark, the 11-year-old
boy, suffered from a football injury to his hip
and could only move about with a wheelchair or
crutches, and that the same injury limited his

ability to move about in his bed. He needed
assistance to turn over in his bed, and indeed
was most likely to have slept on his back. When
this corpse was found by the police he lay on his
stomach, his head buried in a pillow. Ronald DeFeo
fired almost point blank into both boys' backs from
a position standing alongside, somewhat to the
rear of their beds. Both were lying face down
in their beds, and the death bullets came to rest
in the mattresses beneath their bodies. Later
DeFeo described to homicide detectives how he
watched as his brother's foot twitched until it
stopped.

Here again you will find no definitive evidence
indicating whether either or both of these boys
awakened prior to being murdered by DeFeo. Only
the inference that may arise upon considering
the limitations of Mark's injury and the evidence
that these victims four and five were also found
laying face down in death. We will, however, offer
proof indicating that the last victim, Dawn DeFeo,
may very well have awakened in her third floor
bedroom as the Defendant moved toward the stairs.

America's Most Proclaimed Haunted Places

The Testimony of Ronald DeFeo, Jr.

163   R. DeFeo, for Defendant - direct

Q   Ronnie, were you using drugs that day or --

A   That day? No, sir. -

Q   Had you used drugs before that day, within the
last week?

A   No, I didn't use no drugs, no, sir. Not the
kind of drugs you're talking about.

Q   Well, were you taking medication?

A   I was taking medication, you know, from the
drugstore, that my mother gave me, not street drugs.

Q   Ronnie, will you continue as to what you recall
happening.

A   Well, I remember somebody -- I told you I blacked
out or fell asleep. Somebody came down there and start
kicking me. And when I got up the T.V. was off, the
lamp was off, the room was pretty dark. All I know is
somebody was standing there with a rifle in their hands
and the hands that the person had were black.

Q   Ronnie, who was the person?

A   I thought it was my sister.

Q   Who?

A   Dawn. That's who I thought it was, to be quite
honest about it. And I remember there was some conversation

27

about this here, and she said she was going to kill everybody.

I remember taking the rifle away from her. And
when I took the rifle away from her, I don't remember
where I went exactly, back in the sitting room or out
in the hallway, she seemed to disappear. I remember
taking the rifle from there and going to my mother and
father's room with it.

I walked in the door. I didn't go that far
in the door, a couple of feet, maybe. And I just started
to shoot. I don't know if it was three times or four
times, but I started to shoot the gun, fire the gun.

Q   Ronnie, as you were shooting the gun, did you hear
the noise of the rifle?

A   No, sir, that gun didn't make any noise. There
was no noise in the house. It was no lights on at that
time, as far as I remember. The only light that was on
was the bathroom next to Allison's room, they left that
light on in that bathroom. That was the only light I
remember being on on that floor.

And after I shot my mother and father I put
the gun down and left it on the floor. I went back in

the sitting room. I sat down in the chair. The next
thing I know I heard --

      MR. SULLIVAN: Judge, can we suspend for
a minute. I can't get this.

      THE COURT: All right.

      MR. SULLIVAN: Judge, I am going to request
that the last minute or so be read back. I
missed a lot of this.

      THE COURT: All right, read back the entire
answer.

      (Whereupon, the last question and answer
were read back by the Reporter.)

      THE COURT: All right, continue your answer.

A   (Continuing) I was sitting in the sitting room,
and the next thing I heard, it didn't sound like it was
close, it sounded like it was real real far away. I
heard shots going on, gun shots. And when I did get up
to look, I could have sworn it was my sister that came
out of that room and ran up the stairs with a rifle in
her hand. And --

Q   What did you do then, Ronnie?

A   Well, this whole time I was very very calm,

through all of this. I wasn't mad, I was completely calm.
I know I ran -- walked up the stairs, excuse me, walked
up the stairs and I went upstairs. And when I got up
there I believe that I saw Dawn loading the rifle. But
the light was on in her room, that light was on in her
bedroom.

I remember seeing her loading the rifle. And
I remember fighting with her. I know I wanted to throw
her out the window of her bedroom. That was on the third
floor, it was pretty high. I was going to throw her out
the window, but I didn't throw her out the window.

I remember pushing her down into her bed and,
somehow, I don't remember what point of time I got the
gun, but I remember pushing her down. Whether I had the
gun at that time or not I don't know. And I shot her.

Q   What did you do after that, Ronnie?

A   Well --

MR. SULLIVAN: Can we suspend for a minute,
Judge?

THE COURT: All right.

MR. SULLIVAN: Thank you.

THE COURT: Go ahead, Mr. Weber.

The question was what did you do after that.

A   (Continuing) Well, after that I heard footsteps. When I came out of the room, I could have sworn I saw somebody else running down the stairs. So I ran down the stairs. When I got down to the first floor, the front door was open. And I went out the front door. I might have been on the stoop and went as far as the drive-way in the front of my house. I saw somebody or something running across the Ireland's front lawn. That's what I believe did happen in that house. Whether or not it's my imagination or my mind is playing tricks on me, I don't know. You told me it was my imagination.

        MR. SULLIVAN: I will object to that and ask
    that it be stricken.

        THE COURT: Yes, the last statement will
    be stricken.

Q   What did you do after that?

A   Well, after that I went back in the house. I closed the door. I went back upstairs. I don't remember what I did first or what had happened. I know I took a shower. But I think the first thing I did was I cleaned the place up. The place was a mess. There was garbage

America's Most Proclaimed Haunted Places

The Official Statement of the Medical Examiner

Daily News, Chief Mellon, and Lieutenant Richmond of the
Suffolk County Police Department in your office on or about
the afternoon of November 14, 1974, wherein you stated to
those gentlemen that you have total mystification as to how
the six DeFeos could have been killed by a single gunman?

    A   At that time, yes.

        MR. WEBER: Thank you very much. No further
questions.

        MR. SULLIVAN: I have one final.

        THE COURT: All right.

FURTHER REDIRECT EXAMINATION BY MR. SULLIVAN:

    Q   Is your opinion any different now than it was at
the time that you said that?

    A   No.

        MR. SULLIVAN: No further questions.

FURTHER RECROSS EXAMINATION BY MR. WEBER:

    Q   You are still mystified, Doctor?

    A   Yes.

        MR. WEBER: Thank you.

        THE COURT: Doctor, I'd like to establish
basically the time span of the various post-mortem
examinations. Apparently the first one was at one--
around two a.m., and they ran for over a period of

Affidavit from William Davidge: Dawn De'Feo's Boyfriend at the Time of the Murders

SWORN AFFIDAVIT

STATE OF FLORIDA
COUNTY OF

I WILLIAM DAVIDGE, being duly sworn deposes and says:

1. I am affiant and make this affidavit voluntarily and freely regarding **Dawn De'Feo and Ronald De'Feo Jr.**

2. I am **33** years of age,I reside at:

3. That I was the boyfriend of **Dawn De'Feo** and I am a friend of **Ronald De'Feo Jr.** and I was friends with the rest of the **De'Feo** family.

4. That I have direct knowledge about **Dawn De'Feo**, as she was in love with me and wanted to come to Florida to live with me, but her mother, **Louse De'Feo** and father **Ronald De'Feo Sr.**, forbid her from doing so, which led up to hostile incidents between **Dawn** and her mother and father over all this, and **Dawn** was determined to come to Florida, no matter what.

5. I have direct knowledge that **Dawn De'Feo** was using drugs, L.S.D., and mescaline from time to time, and about **Dawn**'s bad temper, which got out of hand on occasions.

6. I have direct knowledge of **Dawn**'s hatred towards her mother and father, and how **Dawn**'s only use for "**Butch**" (Ronald De'Feo, Jr.), was to use him, as "**Butch**" (Ronnie Jr.), gave **Dawn** money that she requested from him. "**Butch**", Ronnie Jr., even gave me **William Davidge**, money to take **Dawn** to her High School Prom, but **Dawn**'s only use for "**Butch**", Ronnie Jr., was to use him.

7. I have direct knowledge of **Dawn**'s attitude right up to the begining of November 1974, as per my phone conversations with her from Florida to Amityville.

Wherefore, the above is true and correct to the best of this affiants personal knowledge.

WILLIAM DAVIDGE

Sworn to before me this
_2_ day of ___July___----1990

THEODORE YURACK
NOTARY PUBLIC, State of New York
M751630
Qualified in Suffolk County

Ronald DeFeo, Jr. was found guilty of all six charges of murder on November 21, 1975, just over one year after the senseless murders of his family. He was remanded to the jail where he would await sentencing on December 4th. On December 4th, the Justice of the Supreme Court, Thomas M. Stark, would find Ronald DeFeo Jr. guilty on all six of the murders. His sentence was one-hundred-forty years without the possibility of parole.

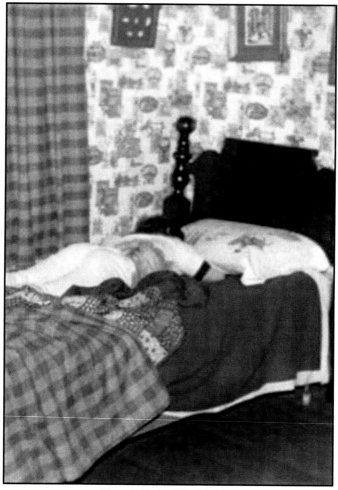

Figure 2. Body of Mark De'Feo.

Figure 3. Body of Dawn De'Feo.

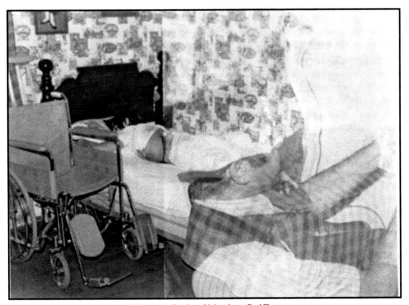

Figure 4. Body of Matthew De'Feo.

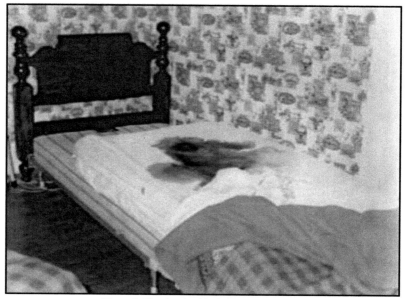

Figure 5. Blood-stained bed of Matthew De'Feo.

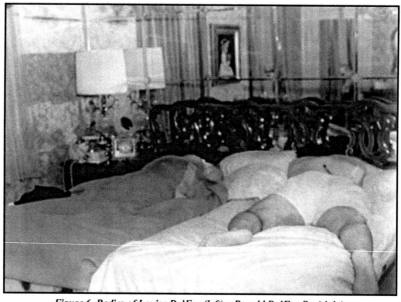

Figure 6. Bodies of Louise De'Feo (left) a Ronald De'Feo Sr. (right).

36

Figure 7. Blood-stained bed of Mark De'Feo.

Figure 8. Body of Allison De'Feo.

37

Figure 9. Funeral of the De'Feo family.

Many say for me to put these photos in my book is tacky. I argue they are indeed a major part of the truth behind the brutal crimes Ronald Defeo committed. In particular, it is the photos of the children that tell the story of a cold-blooded killer: A person who holds no respect for a human life. The names and ages of the victims are as follows: Ronald Defeo Sr. age 43, Louise Defeo age 42, Dawn Terese Defeo age 18, Allison Louise DeFeo age 13, Mark Gregory DeFeo age 12, and John Matthew DeFeo age 9

While Ronald DeFeo was on trial, his family was put to rest at St. Charles Cemetery. Ronald was denied permission to attend the funeral by the courts. Throughout the trial, and to this day, Ronald, Jr. claims he did not murder his whole family. He claims Dawn killed their father. According to the evidence in the court records, it was indeed possible Ronald did not act alone. The court transcripts can be brought up through public records out of Suffolk County.

America's Most Proclaimed Haunted Places

Today, Ronald Defeo's wife stands by him.

It seemed the town's people of Amityville could now get back to living their quaint, quiet little lives. The town did indeed survive the horror that besieged their quiet little town. With Ronald DeFeo, Jr. finally behind bars and the house at 112 Ocean Avenue now on the market, life within the town could finally settle back down and move on. Or so they thought. Not long after that the town would be turned upside down once again.

George and Kathy Lutz bought the DeFeo house at 112 Ocean Avenue for eighty thousand dollars. A steal as eighty thousand was way below the fair market value. And for the Lutz's, it was the house of their dreams. Even though the Realtor informed them the house was once the grisly site of a mass murder, the Lutz's were unconcerned. The closing price was just too good to walk away from. Just over one year after the murders, George and Kathy Lutz along with their three children moved into the house. It was December 18th, only fourteen days after Ronald Defeo was sentenced to one-hundred-forty years.

George Lutz owned a construction company. Shortly after purchasing the home, his company started going under. The house payments soon became too much to handle. Now the fun part of the Lutz's story began.

It has been reported Kathy Lutz claimed to feel an evil presence on the first day of moving into the house. She claimed to have called Father Ray Pecoraro and had him come over to bless the house. She claimed that while he did so, a voice of "pure evil" commanded him to get out. As he fled the house, he advised Kathy to leave immediately, stating that indeed there was an evil within the house. However, the Lutz's had everything tied up within the house and would not be able to survive the loss they would suffer if they were to sell the home.

So, according to the Lutzs' as the days went on, the house came to life. An unbearable cold took over the house and not even the fireplace seemed to take the edge off of the chill within the house. The youngest child started to see the face of a pig in her bedroom window; a pig she called "Jody". George Lutz began having visions of walking through the house, late at night, with a shotgun... Murdering his family and fighting with voices within the dead of night calling to him... Commanding him to kill his family. And always at three-fifteen a.m.

As the days went on, a demonic force attacked the family, turning them on one another. On more than one occasion, the children's beds banged against the floor as they cried out for help. The cross Kathy hung within the house was found mysteriously turned upside down. After only twenty-eight days, on December 23rd, the Lutz family left the house at 112 Ocean Avenue claiming never to return.

Okay, now the real deal…

George indeed got in way over his head with the payments of a house out of their realistic budget. Shortly after purchasing the home, George Lutz's company took a turn for the worse, and he needed a way out. The same attorney who represented Ronald Defeo was a friend of the Lutz's. He came up with the plan to get the Lutz's out of a house they should have never have purchased in the first place.

One night, over several bottles of wine, he told the Lutz's the story Ronald had told. And with that the Amityville horror was born. The Lutz's did indeed leave the house after twenty-eight days, but only four days later on December 27th, the Lutz's returned to the house and held a yard sale. They then moved to California and started over.

There have been some unexplained things taking place within the house at 112 Ocean Avenue. The first being the family who moved into the house right after the Lutz's had a son die in the same room once belonging to the two youngest DeFeo boys. The cause of death was never found.

And as for George Lutz, he died of a heart attack not too long ago. Kathy still stands by her statement that the story was given life over a few bottles of wine.

As to Ronald Defeo—well, he still sits in prison, waiting out his one-hundred-forty years. He still claims he did not kill alone, and that Dawn had a hand in the murders. Indeed, that is what I believe after spending two and a half years researching this. He now claims he should have gotten a lighter sentence, since Dawn killed their father. But, the fact remains he undoubtedly killed five people. He killed his own family.

The true sadness of the Amityville Horror is that lives were lost and a town was turned upside down. Do I believe that the police of Suffolk County messed this up? The answer is yes. There is most definitely evidence that has been withheld, truth that has been suppressed, and the actual whole story has never been told. As well as evidence that has been lost or tainted in some way. However, the simple facts remain--Ronald Defeo did indeed kill his family in cold blood and does deserve to be right where he is today. By his own admission he killed at least five members of his family.

I wish I could say this house was and is truly haunted, but it is actually only a great story by one of the masters of horror...from the brilliant mind of Jay Anson.

~ CHAPTER TWO ~

~ Northern State Hospital ~
(*Sedro-Woolley Mental Hospital*)
Sedro-Woolley, Washington

As darkness falls upon the asylum that sits desolate just outside the town hidden within the mountains of Sedro Woolley, Washington, you can hear the screams of those whose spirits still remain within the very walls of the old asylum, trapped forever in a nightmare of days gone by. Dr. Walter Freeman was one of the leading doctors of the frontal-lobe lobotomy. At the time it was a break through surgery believed to cure the insane.

As the wheels of the gurneys rolled down the second floor hallway to the large room with the two way windows, Interns, doctors, and nurses alike, looked in on the patients bound with leather straps on their hands and feet. A crude leather strap was, at times, placed over the forehead of patients and was often used in association with nurses and other staff members holding the patients down to further restrain them before turning the electric shock machine to high and administering it until the patients were rendered unconscious.

America's Most Proclaimed Haunted Places

As Doctor Freeman took up a tool, much like that of an old time ice pick, he pulled back the eye lids and placed the ice pick up into the lobe. Using a small hammer he then punched holes through the temples and one within the center through the nose. But maybe the most famous story of all lies within the tunnels beneath the hospital itself. Reportedly, within the walls of the tunnels lay a laboratory; a laboratory where Doctor Freeman was rumored to keep some of the heads along with other body parts in formaldehyde. This was a room only he had known about. But many who worked with him suspected there was such a place. Shortly before the hospital closed, Doctor Freeman died taking with him the truth of what actually lies within the tunnels of Northern State Hospital.

The old hospital now sits vacant, only holding passing memories of times best forgotten long ago. All power to the old hospital has long since been cut off and the wires that once carried the power to the hospital torn down. Even now, some nights, lights can be seen on the second floor of the building and the cries of countless many are still heard today on a moonless night.

Sedro Woolley is indeed one of the most proclaimed haunted hospitals around today. It's a place that, to this day, hides many secrets of days long passed. Hidden amongst the ruins is a graveyard containing upwards of one thousand bodies, many of which are the unclaimed and forgotten. Could it be those forgotten who still roam the halls of the large hospital? Could the man in the white lab-coat be the spirit of Doctor Freeman, himself?

Okay, now the real deal…

In 2005, I was lucky enough to have a first hand glimpse inside the walls of this extremely haunted hospital, alongside one of the most renowned teams in the paranormal field today. TAPS traveled to Northern State and was given the opportunity to walk the very halls within the large hospital. I was given the chance to walk the very steps Dr. Freeman walked in those tunnels underneath the old hospital. But, as for the laboratory, it had long ago been put to rest and cleared out of all once hidden within it. While I was there, a man named Ray, a gentle man who once worked at the hospital when it was operational, told me the story of the laboratory.

As I sat, he told me that a few years after the hospital closed, they ran across the laboratory Dr. Freeman kept hidden for so many years. As they cleared it out, they took everything in it to the land-fill. Everything except the bodies parts, (or so they thought), for fear they would release a disease from years passed. The laboratory was then sealed shut. Several days later, a large rain storm blew in, as it always does in Seattle and the land-fill flooded. The large, unopened metal containers brought there only days earlier, opened. Body parts ended up in people's yards. In the beginning, the police were on the hunt for a serial killer. But eventually, they discovered the body parts indeed came from the hospital. The formaldehyde they were stored in preserved them so well; the body parts never decompose. But it was what he told me next that turned my very blood cold.

Ray shared with me: "Late at night, when all is quiet on the campus, I often see lights on within the old hospital. Even with the power lines long down due to a big storm that took out most of the power poles carrying the power to the old hospital, I could still see them."

As dusk set in, I would come to find out exactly what Ray was talking about. Just as we were getting ready to leave, the lights within the old hospital came on. It was at that time I got in touch with WISPERS: a TAPS family team. The next day I returned with

WISPERS for another walk through of the old hospital. At this time while in the hospital, I got the overwhelming feeling some one, or some thing, watched my every move. It was the feeling that whatever happened there so long ago, never really ended.

However, it was in the surgery room, where I found my head starting to feel like it was going to explode and the very breath within my body somehow absent. As the darkness threatened to take me over, I left the old hospital, never to return again.

Shortly after that, they called in some paranormal investigators by the name of TAPS. A team out of Rhode Island, who at the time was on their second or third season of a TV show call "Ghost Hunters". They did what I would not have done, not at that place any way. What they found would turn the paranormal community, and indeed, the world upside down! They caught a full body apparition running down the hall once housing the surgery room—

Figure 10. I'd like to dedicate this section to Ray. As it was Ray who started me on this journey in 2005. It was with the kindest man I have ever met, that I walked these halls. He will be greatly missed.

Figure 11. Northern state Hospital shortly after opening.

Figure 12. Northern State Hospital opening day on May 25, 1912. The horses and buggies brought the town's people from all over to marvel at the large, first of its kind, self-sufficient insane asylum.

Figure 13. Student's Dorm.

Figure 14. Nurses station, 2nd floor, opening day.

Figure 15. The old surgery room as it sits today.

Figure 16. The main entrance as it is today.

48

Figure 17. An old patient's room.

where Doctor Freeman performed so many of the Trans lobal frontal lobotomies. It was not until much later I would come to find out about this.

As I looked upon this building, a feeling of sadness came over me. To this day, I still am not sure why. Whether it is the thought of so many lives lost, or the stories I had just heard of what took place within this building, I do not know. Whatever it was...it still sticks with me today.

Biography of Dr. Walter Freeman

Born November 14, 1895 ~ Died May 31, 1972 (aged 76)
Born in Philadelphia, Pennsylvania, USA
Profession ~ Physician, Psychiatrist,
Specialism ~ psychosurgery, neurology

America's Most Proclaimed Haunted Places

Known for performing lobotomies, Popularized the "Ice Pick"
Lobotomies

Education~ Yale University, Pennsylvania School of Medicine

Dr. Walter Freeman followed in the footsteps of his father who was a successful doctor and in the footsteps of his grandfather, William Keen, the president of the American Medical Association. In 1944-1945, Dr. Walter Freeman was the President of the American Board of Psychiatry and Neurology. Freeman performed nearly three thousand-five hundred Lobotomies, on record any way. It is unknown just how many he actually did while perfecting the lobotomy as you will see later on in this narrative. It was from Amarro Flaubert that Dr. Freeman took the Trans-orbital lobotomy and began to perfect it. His procedure quickly became known as the "Ice Pick" Lobotomy, nicknamed as such due to the appearance of his chosen tool resembling an ice pick, also called a leucotomy.

The first actual "ice picks" used were out of Dr. Freeman's kitchen. He began performing surgeries on brains in the hospital morgue late at night. He would reportedly sneak in when no one was around. His first actual patient in 1936 was a sixty-three year old female. Her name was Alice Hood Hammatt, whom he rendered unconscious by electric shock. Then he took the ice pick out and peeled back her eye lids, shoving the ice pick beneath the eyelid. The first one, shown here, was when Dr. Freeman drilled six holes in her brain.

Alice did survive. This gave Dr. Freeman a rush and soon he became hungry for fame. He became known as the *Ice Pick Lobotomist*. Dr. Freeman used the electro-on-valise therapy machine as a drugless general anesthesia. The electro-on-valise therapy machine caused electrical current to pass through the patient's brain and produced a convulsive seizure. After the seizure stopped, the patient would be in a temporarily induced comatose state for from four to five minutes, which is all it took to perform the lobotomies.

Figure 18. (Left) Portrait of Dr. Walter Freeman

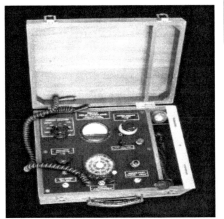

Figure 19. (Right) Image of Dr. Walter Freeman performing a surgical procedure.

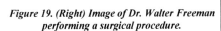

Figure 20. (left) This instrument is believed to be the very same model machine Dr. Freeman used.

America's Most Proclaimed Haunted Places

Dr. Freeman worked at Northern State Hospital during its peak. The hospital maintained a graveyard, set off in the back, for the patients who had no family. It was often said there are over one thousand unmarked graves behind Northern State Hospital. But until 2007 it was unsure just how many truly existed. The count is three thousand-two hundred today. Markers sit on the numerous gravesites and, today, even the unclaimed graves are marked. Voices from the dead have now been heard.

To this day the old hospital building serves as a job corp. The stories that Sedro-Woolley is haunted have been told by many who lived there. There are also stories of a man who walks the halls, late at night, often standing within the room of those who live there. Another sighting is of a small girl skipping down the hall.

The photos caught even today by so many are, to say the least, impressive. In fact, it was these photos which got me digging into the death records of the ones who passed away there. Also at the same time I found the Northern State Hospital did house children at one point in time. Although I have not been able to verify this through documentation, I was told by Ray that often the children would come with the mother, if the father or another relative was unable to take them. He spoke of Mary, who would often run up and down the halls of the old hospital. She was, in his words, 'about five or six years old'. She fell ill and passed away in the old hospital. Could it be Mary who remains there today?

There are no death records to support this claim that I have located in the years I've been researching Northern State Hospital. But, I also found that not all who have died within the walls of the old hospital are listed in the town's death records. One thing is sure though, I have traveled all over in search for the truth of the most proclaimed haunted places. This is, indeed, one place I would not return to for an overnight stay. For what I saw within those walls, I still don't know how to explain. To this day, I carry the images with me in my nightmares. The tall figure of the man who followed us the day we were there just as the sun was to give way to the darkness was something I have not experienced in any other place. The sheer feeling of the touch on my back was more than even I care to think about. Whatever lies with in the walls of the old hospital is indeed left over from a time long best forgotten and buried forever.

~ CHAPTER THREE ~

~ Starvation Heights ~
Location not provided.

Back in 1906, a female doctor named Linda Hazzard, moved to the small town of Olalla, in the mountains of Seattle, Washington, not far from where the old Northern State Hospital sits. Linda Hazzard was the first doctor to receive a degree as a "fasting specialist" within the United States. Known for her "homeopathic medicines," she believed she could cure all illnesses without using the medications many hospitals and sanitariums were using at the time. Dr. Hazzard's theory was that any disease could be cured by fasting, also known as starving the body for weeks, sometimes even months on end. Her beliefs led her straight to a court in which she found herself being tried as a serial killer.

In 1909, Dr Linda Hazzard settled into the town of Olalla, Washington. She and her husband bought a forty acre piece of land so Linda could realize her dream of opening a Sanitarium, the first of its kind. It has been stated Dr. Linda Hazzard starved her patients, believing it would cure them of any illness. However, most of them did not make it out of the Sanitarium. As they starved to death, one by one, she convinced her patients to sign over everything they owned to her. As they each passed, one by one, she placed their bodies in a shallow grave and planted a tree atop them. When she ran out of room to bury the dead, she simply began to have them thrown off the cliff behind the Sanitarium, then claimed all their worldly possessions as her own.

The most renowned of all the stories is that of two very wealthy British sisters who were sent to her Sanitarium, aptly nicknamed *Starvation Heights*, Their names were Dora and Claire Williamson. Their family had heard the news there was a cure for all illnesses, without the use of medication. Soon, the two sisters found themselves at *Starvation Heights*, far away from their home and all the people they knew and loved. As the days went by, there was no contact from the sisters to their family. Until Dora finally made a desperate plea to a close friend, begging them to come from Australia and save them. This disturbing plea for help caused great worry for their father, especially since the sisters had always kept in close contact with their family. By the time help arrived, it was too late for Claire, who in May of 1911, lost her life. Claire's death proved to be the saving grace for her sister, Dora.

Figure 21. (left) Portrait of Dr. Linda Hazzard.

Figure 22. (right) This photo of Dora Williamson was taken only a few days before her rescue.

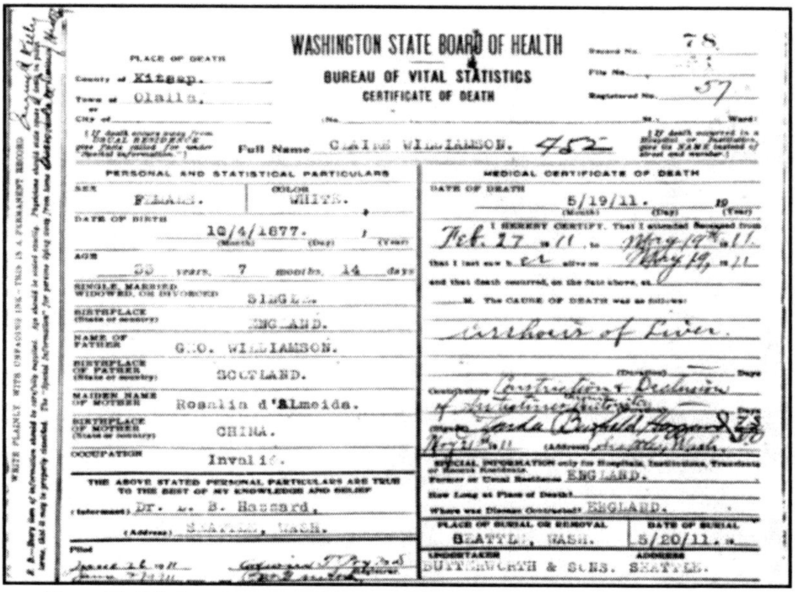
WASHINGTON STATE BOARD OF HEALTH
BUREAU OF VITAL STATISTICS
CERTIFICATE OF DEATH

Record No. 78
Registered No. 57

PLACE OF DEATH
County of Kitsap.
Town of Olalla.

Full Name Claire Williamson. 452

PERSONAL AND STATISTICAL PARTICULARS
Sex: Female.
Color: White.
Date of Birth: 10/4/1877.
Age: 33 years 7 months 14 days
Single, Married, Widowed, or Divorced: Single.
Birthplace: England.
Name of Father: Geo. Williamson.
Birthplace of Father: Scotland.
Maiden Name of Mother: Rosalia d'Almeida.
Birthplace of Mother: China.
Occupation: Invalid.
THE ABOVE STATED PERSONAL PARTICULARS ARE TRUE TO THE BEST OF MY KNOWLEDGE AND BELIEF
(Informant) Dr. L. B. Hazzard.

MEDICAL CERTIFICATE OF DEATH
Date of Death: 5/19/11.
I HEREBY CERTIFY, That I attended deceased from Feb. 27 '11 to May 19th '11
that I last saw her alive on May 19, '11
and that death occurred, on the date stated above, at
The CAUSE OF DEATH was as follows:
Cirrhosis of Liver.
Contributory: Constriction & Occlusion of Intestinal tract
(Signed) Linda Burfield Hazzard
May 21st '11 (Address) Seattle, Wash.
SPECIAL INFORMATION only for Hospitals, Institutions, Transients or Recent Residents.
Former or Usual Residence: England.
How Long at Place of Death?
Where was Disease Contracted? England.
Place of Burial or Removal: Seattle, Wash.
Date of Burial: 5/20/11.
Undertaker / Address: Butterworth & Sons. Seattle.

Figure 23. This is a photocopy of the actual death certificate for Dora's sister, Claire Williamson.

One must remember that Claire Williamson was not the only victim who suffered at the hands of Dr. Linda Hazzard. The names below are just some of her many victims:

(1908) - Daisy Maud Haglund, Ida Wilcox

(1909) - Blanche B. Tindall, Viola Heaton, Eugene Stanley Wakelin (*the one victim who died of a gunshot to the head*)

(1910) - Maude Whitney, Earl Edward Erdman

(1911) - Frank Southard, C.A. Harrison, Ivan Ellsworth Rader, Claire Williamson

Dr. Linda Hazzard soon found herself in the midst of a murder trial; a trial that would leave the little town of Olalla in complete shock. The small courthouse, shown in the photograph below, had never seen anything like this before.

America's Most Proclaimed Haunted Places

The trial of Dr. Linda Hazzard lasted for three weeks, during which, each day the judge admonished Dr. Linda Hazzard for coaching and intimidating the defense witnesses. On February 4, 1912, the trial came to an end. Dr. Linda Hazzard was convicted of manslaughter and sentenced to two to twenty years of hard labor in the Walla-Walla penitentiary. Only eight short years later, Linda Hazzard returned to the town of Olalla, and built her dream sanitarium. This time, she opened it as a School of Health as her license to practice medicine had been stripped from her. The town, however, would not let what Linda Hazzard had done be forgotten. The town aptly named the school of health, *Starvation Heights.*

This is the only photo I found of her school. According to the Olalla archives, it is the only one in existence. *Starvation Heights* burned to the ground in 1935. It was never rebuilt. In 1938, Dr. Linda Hazzard died of, you guessed it, starvation. It was thought

Figure 24. This is the actual courthouse where the doctor's trial took place.

Figure 25. Dr. Linda Hazzard's School of Health.

that much of the history and the photo records of *Starvation Heights* were lost forever. In fact it was while I lived in Washington and worked on the Northern State portion of this book that I came across *Starvation Heights*. I wish I was able to give you more on this place, but I just cannot. But having said that, know this; there is a great book out on this place, *"Starvation Heights"* authored by Gregg Olsen. I have not read it but have heard nothing but good about it.

~ CHAPTER FOUR ~

~ Fort Morgan ~
Gulf Shores, Alabama

It was in August of 2009, that I found myself at the old fort. As I pulled up to the large fort, it felt as if I stepped back in time. It seemed almost as if the old fort still sat waiting for the next set of troops to take up residence within those very walls. As night fell upon the old fort, it seemed as if we were transported back in time, to a day long forgotten. On the first night, as the teams set up within the old room known only to us as the boy scout room, it would not be long before a large shadow figure made its presence known to all. It seemed to be fascinated by those of us who came to hear the stories from those who had lived there once, so long ago.

It would not be the only voice from the past that would reach out to the paranormal teams who had come to embark on the old fort.

On the first night, as I sat in on my first box session, I learned that what I once believed was outside the realm of possibility was indeed possible. Not only were the voices of those who died there

Figure 26. Cornerstone of Fort Morgan.

one-hundred-forty-five years ago still very much there, but we were even capable of an intelligent dialogue with them. The disk provided to you with this book contains some of the EVP's and the very words we heard during our time spent at the fort.

The History of Fort Morgan

After the war of 1812, the United States (US) started a program to strengthen its seacoast defenses. In 1818, the US contracted out the building of the fort to Benjamin Hopkins of Vermont. It was roughly a year later, when Benjamin Hopkins would fall ill of the yellow fever. He died after accomplishing very little on the fort.

The US then brought in another contractor, Samuel Hawkins, from New York. But, like the first contractor, Samuel died as work was being done on the fort. At the time of his death in 1821, he, like

Figure 27. The first night outside what we came to know as the Boy Scout room.

Figure 28. My first box session with Blaine and CC.

Figure 29. This photograph was taken in1864, showing the damage done to the south side of the fort. This fort was named in honor of Daniel Morgan.

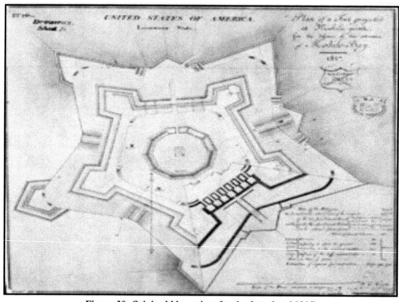

Figure 30. Original blue prints for the fort, dated 1817.

his predecessor before him, also accomplished very little.

After the deaths of the first two contractors, the US Army turned the task of building the fort over to the Corps of Engineers under R.E. DeRussey. At this time, DeRussey used slaves to build the fort, often paying the owner for the use of their slaves, as the Army could not own slaves. The owners of the slaves were not only paid for their slaves' work, but the value of the slaves increased as they learned a skilled trade. Following the paths of the first contractors, many of the slaves died during the construction of the fort.

In 1825, once again, the fort claimed another victim. Captain DeRussey fell ill and turned the job of constructing the fort over to his Deputy Lieutenant Cornelius Ogden. Ogden completed the fort in March of 1834. The fort was then turned over to F.S Belton; the Commander of Company B, 2nd US Artillery. The unit remained at the fort for about a year and a half, before their transfer to Florida to assist in the second Seminole Indian war. On January 3, 1861, just before dawn, John B. Todd captured the fort.

Figure 31. On August 22, General Richard Page quoted, "I am prepared to sacrifice life and will only surrender when I have no means of defense."

Figure 32. This image was taken just days after the fort was surrendered.

Figure 33. The extensive battle on the fort left much damage to it and the lighthouse.

Figure 34. The above image and the following excerpt is one of the last entries in Page's diary.

The Defense of Fort Morgan:
The Report of Brig. Gen. Richard L. Page,
Commander of the Fort

"*Early on the morning of the 5th of August, 1864, I observed unusual activity in the Federal fleet off Mobile Bay, indicating, as I supposed, that they were about to attempt the passage of the fort. After an early breakfast the men were sent to the guns. Everybody was in high spirits. In a short time preparations were ended, and then followed perfect silence, before the noise of battle.*

At 6 o'clock A.M. the enemy's ships began to move in with flags flying. They gradually fell into a line, consisting of twenty-three vessels, four of which were monitors. Each of the first four of the largest wooden ships had a smaller one lashed on the side opposite the fort, and was itself protected by a monitor between it and the fort. The smaller ships followed in line.

As they approached with a moderate wind and on the flood tide, I fired the first gun at long range, and soon the firing became general, our fire being briskly returned by the enemy. For a short time the smoke was so dense that the vessels could not be distinguished, but still the firing was incessant.

When abreast of the fort the leading monitor, the Tecumseh, suddenly sank. Four of the crew swam ashore and a few others were picked up by a boat from the enemy. Cheers from the garrison now rang out, which were checked at once, and the order was passed to sink the admiral's ship and then cheer.

At this moment the Brooklyn, the leading ship, stopped her engine, apparently in doubt; whereupon the order was passed to concentrate on her, in the hope of sinking her, my belief being that it was the admiral's ship, the Hartford. As I learned afterward, he was on the second ship. Farragut's coolness and quick perception saved the fleet from great disaster and probably from destruction. While the Brooklyn hesitated, the admiral put his helm to starboard, sheered outside the Brooklyn, and took the lead, the rest following, thus saving the fouling and entanglement of the vessels and the danger of being sunk under my guns. When, after the fight, the Brooklyn was sent to Boston for repairs, she was found to have been struck over seventy times in her hull and masts, as was shown by a drawing that was sent me while I was a prisoner of war at Fort Lafayette.

The ships continued passing rapidly by, no single vessel being under fire more than a few moments. Shot after shot was seen to strike, and shells to explode, on or about the vessels, but their sides being heavily protected by chain cables, hung along the sides and abreast the engines, no vital blow could be inflicted, particularly as the armament of the fort consisted of guns inadequate in caliber and numbers for effective service against a powerful fleet in rapid motion. The torpedoes in the channel were also harmless; owing to the depth of the water, the strong tides, and the imperfect moorings none exploded..."

(This excerpt was taken from the original on location in the Ft. Morgan history museum)

So, even though I shared the place with countless spiders, (and consequently was bitten causing me to become very ill) along with numerous snakes, I would go back in a heartbeat. This is one of the only places I have found that when you ask a question, they will answer you. And not just once in a while, but every single time. The EVPs caught were throughout the entire anniversary that we were there for. On the disk you will be able to hear just what we did and some of the numerous EVPs caught in different locations of the fort.

Today, the fort still seems to be alive with the past. The old fort still stands, as if time itself has simply passed it by.

Figure 35. The tunnel that leads to the center of the fort- off to the left is the old hospital room. This is where the paranormal team, SAPS, caught a lot of their EVP's.

Figure 36. Interior photo of the fort.

Figure 37. As you first enter the old fort

America's Most Proclaimed Haunted Places

Figure 38. Outside walls of the fort.

Figure 39. This sits isolated, as a permanent reminder of the loss involved with this place.

70

Figure 40. The old canon still stands guard.

Figure 41. Another photo of the outside walls of the fort.

Figure 42. Colonnaded interior photo of the fort.

Figure 43. The old jail at night.

Figure 44. Interior photo of the fort.

Figure 45. Interior photo of the fort.

Figure 46. Interior photo of the fort.

Figure 47. Interior photo of the fort.

Figure 48. Interior photo of the fort.

Figure 49. Interior photo of the fort.

Figure 50. Interior photo of the fort.

Figure 51. Interior photo of the fort.

Figure 52. Interior photo of the fort.

Figure 53. Interior photo of the fort.

Figure 54. Interior photo of the fort.

Figure 55. Interior photo of the fort.

Figure 56. Interior photo of the fort.

Figure 57. This was the room where most of the woman got touched or had their hair pulled—better known to all as the Boom Room. True recent documented history tells us of a man who died in an explosion in this room while disassembling some of the old ammo.

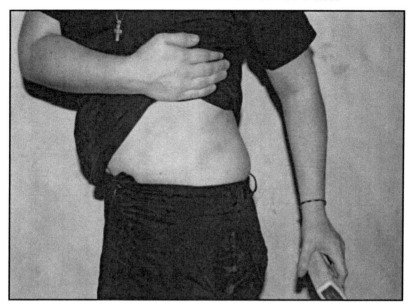

Figures 58 & 59. It was as many others sat within the room that out of nowhere this paranormal team member got scratched by something no one could see. This was the room, as well, that on the 145th anniversary of the bloodiest battle to take place at the old fort, we all heard loud booms erupting just outside the room.

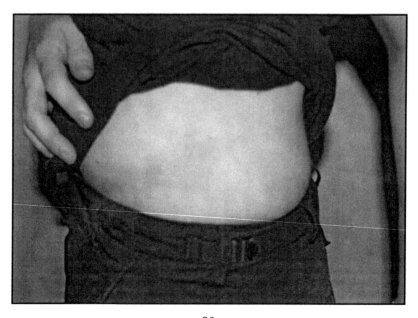

Figure 60. Interior photo of the fort.

Figure 61. The inner walls of the fort.

Figure 62. Interior photo of the fort.

Figure 63. Interior photo of the fort.

~ CHAPTER FIVE ~

~ Waverly Hills Sanatorium ~
Southwestern Louisville County, Kentucky

Many of us have heard the stories of the spirits that, to this day, still take up residence in the old Sanatorium. Various paranormal teams claim Waverly Hills is one of the most haunted places in America. It is indeed one of the most active paranormal hot spots known today. Every year, thousands of paranormal investigators and hundreds of paranormal teams come to Waverly in hopes of capturing some evidence to help them justify this claim and bring validation to the paranormal world. And Waverly Hills always seems to deliver just that. It has been documented on numerous occasions, especially on the fourth floor, many paranormal teams have been attacked, sometimes violently. This has been seen on several well known, paranormal, television shows including "Most Haunted."

The History of Waverly Hills

Tuberculosis ran rampant at the time in Waverly Hills. During

83

the height of the epidemic, doctors frantically struggled to find a cure. For a brief period of time, especially at Waverly Hills, it was believed sunlight might be the cure. For the most part, all of the attempted treatments at the time were just short of barbaric. In most cases, the patient's chest was cracked opened and their lungs exposed to the ultraviolet light of the sun. The theory being that the sunlight would stop the spread of the bacteria significant with TB.

Sometimes, even in the dead of a harsh Kentucky winter, the patients would be left lying, chest opened, lungs exposed to the outside elements for hours at a time. They also implanted balloons into the patients lungs and filled them with air, often times causing the lung to explode, nearly always fatal.

Figure 64. Exterior photo of Waverly Hills Sanatorium.

America's Most Proclaimed Haunted Places

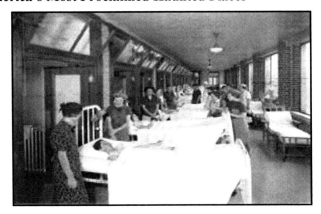

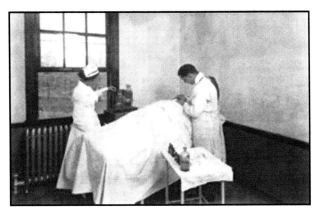

Figures 65,66 & 67. These photos are of Waverly Hills at the height of the tuberculosis epidemic.

Figure 68. The roof was mostly used for the children. They would often be taken up to play in the sun light.

In the late 1800's, Major Hays descended on Louisville, Kentucky with his family. At the time, there was only vast land and he was in need of a school to send his daughters to. In 1883, Major Hays had a one room school built and hired a local teacher by the name of Miss Harris. This school was named "Waverly Hills". Major Hays loved the name and named the very land, Waverly Hills. With tuberculosis fast becoming an epidemic in Kentucky, the need became apparent to isolate the infected from the rest of the population. A small hospital was built with enough room to hold forty to fifty patients. But, as the epidemic continued to spread, the hospital, like most at that time, was soon well over capacity, having one-hundred-forty patients at once.

In 1926, the hospital along with the surrounding land, was bought and the large gothic style hospital which stands today was built. The new hospital was built to hold a capacity of four hundred patients at any given time. The hospital functioned as a tuberculosis hospital until 1961, when antibiotics came into play. With the tuberculosis outbreak now better contained, the hospital was closed down for quarantine and renovations. It reopened in 1962 under the name, Woodhaven Medical for the Geriatric.

I would be remiss if I failed to mention the hospital had seen at least seven-thousand-seven-hundred and two horrific deaths before it was closed in 1980, not the commonly misquoted sixty-four-thousand deaths said to be attributed to the hospital. In fact, that number is actually the death toll of all Louisville, Kentucky, during the TB outbreak.

It has also been stated that the tunnel that runs under Waverly, and has more recently been nicknamed as "the body chute", was used to take out the bodies of those who passed away, to prevent the other patients knowing of the number of deaths taking place in

Figure 69. It is documented that the dead were removed from Waverly through the "body chute."

the hospital around them. The Doctors, as well as the rest of the staff, felt it was important the patients not see this happening all around them. One of the few kindnesses actually documented at the brutal hospital. This was a rather common practice of the day. Waverly's own "body chute" ran under the entire length of the first floor and all the way to the street outside.

The Stories of Hauntings in Waverly and the Truth Behind Them

One of the most popular, and often repeated stories associated with Waverly and its ghosts, is one of a young girl who wanders the third and fourth floor named "Mary".

I've spent countless hours researching this and did come across a death record of a Mary Ann (age seven). She arrived at Waverly in 1937. She was there for a very short period of time, only days, before her passing. Other then this record, there is no other child by the name of Mary on any record associated with Waverly at or near the time of her rumored death. There is no mention of a last name which leads me to the logical conclusion that she was an orphan at the time of her death. This would be concurrent with many records on orphans in that time period. There's really not much more information known or available about Mary.

The Infamous Room 502

In many movies and even in a few documentaries, it has been reported a nurse took her own life by hanging herself in the room numbered *502*. The stories vary from time to time depending on who is telling it. Some say the woman, being a single pregnant woman, hung herself in fear of what others would think. There is another version of the story saying she contracted tuberculosis. After having been witness to the suffering she would endure, she chose to take her own life rather than undergo the treatment that was being given.

In 1928 after becoming pregnant, a tall dark, haired woman had hung herself. This is well documented in several logs kept by both the doctors and the staff. She was known to often offer her help with the children at Waverly, even taking a special liking to one little boy who had become an orphan when his parents passed away while in the hospital. Not long before the nurse hung herself the boy, known only as Robert in the logs, had passed away. Her name is not mentioned. This death was documented in the *Autobiography of Assistant Medical Director Dr. J Frank W. Stewart.*

There is a lesser known story of a nurse who allegedly jumped to her death from the window of *Room 502.* There is no death

Figure 70. The infamous room 502.

89

record nor ledger entry to support this allegation. However, due to most of the records having been lost or destroyed, I cannot say for sure that a second nurse did not die from jumping off the building. I can nether confirm nor deny the claim at this time.

I have chosen not to spend as much time on Waverly Hills as I have spent on some of the others in this book, as I believe it is over-publicized. Also many of the relevant records that once held the key to discovering the truth have all but been destroyed. Absence of concrete evidence makes it nearly impossible to present irrefutable proof and the documented truth in the history of Waverly Hills. On the other hand, it is indeed a fact that I have been given more EVP's on Waverly than many of the other places within this book. In addition are the many personal experiences, photos, and video footage documented by countless paranormal investigators and ghost hunting enthusiasts. So, for arguments sake, if you asked me if I believed Waverly is haunted, I would say there is indeed something there that does not show as human.

It is a good possibility the ones who lived, suffered, and died within those walls may very well still be there. Without the hard facts and the documented proof found in historical records, I simply cannot make that call. But, I must say, it is a great old building—a building that belongs on the cover of some book. She is indeed breathtaking.

~ CHAPTER SIX ~

~ Metropolitan State Hospital ~
Walthum/Levinytrn/Belmont, Massachusetts

Metropolitan State Hospital was built around 1930. It was built based on the cottage-style, asylum look. With its open space and the vast fields and woods around it, it took on a look of comfort, more so than most of the other large hospitals back in those days. But, like most asylums in that time, it was not long before it was over crowded and beyond capacity, causing patients to be housed in the corridors from time to time. At this time the tunnels, running under most asylums of the time period, was used as the primary entrance and exit of the hospital.

It was not until 1978 that the conditions of the asylum came to light. When one of the patients, Melvin W. Wilson, brutally murdered another patient of the hospital, a woman named Anne Marie Davee, the hospital came under the scrutiny of the public. The horrid conditions in which the patients were housed made it into the news, right alongside the murder. Wilson murdered Anne Marie with a hatchet in the woods surrounding the asylum. Most

Figure 71. Photo showing the exterior of the hospital.

disturbingly, it was discovered later that Melvin Wilson kept seven of Ann's teeth and, one of the nurses found him sitting on the floor of his room playing with them. On August 12th, 1980, Wilson led investigators to three shallow graves that were the burial sights of Davee's dismembered corpse pieces.

Following are some news articles published at the time by the Boston Globe:

Boston Globe Archives
August 12, 1980
George Croft

The dismembered body of a Metropolitan State Hospital patient, missing since 1978 was found buried on the grounds of the Waltham institution today. A former Metropolitan patient, charged with the murder, let police and hospital authorities to the several places in which parts of the body had been buried.

Melvin Wilson, 52, now a patient at Bridgewater State Hospital, was to be arraigned in Waltham District Court today on murder charges in the death of Ann Marie Davee, 36.

Davee had been a patient at various mental institutions in Massachusetts and Maine. She disappeared in August 1978, according to Ken Wayne, a spokesperson for Atty. Gen. Francis X. Bellotti.

State Police detective attached to Bellotti's office intensified their search eight months ago, questioning former patients known to have associated with Davee.

Boston Globe Archives
August 13, 1980
Edward Quill & Jean Dietz

A 57-year-old man is undergoing observation today at Bridgewater State Hospital to determine if he is competent to stand trial after his arraignment in Waltham District Court yesterday on a charge of murdering a woman two years ago. Melvin W. Wilson, who has spent 39 years as a patient in state mental institutions, was returned yesterday to Bridgewater, where he is currently a patient, for 16 days of observation.

America's Most Proclaimed Haunted Places

Psychiatrists will try to determine if Wilson was criminally responsible for the slaying of Ann Marie Davee, 36, whose dismembered body was found yesterday in three shallow graves on a wooded slope near Waltham's Metropolitan State Hospital

Wilson yesterday led police and hospital authorities to the graves in the woods next to the Kathryn Foran Furcolo Building. Davee was murdered "on or about Aug. 9, 1978," police said. Wilson and Davee were patients at the state hospital then.

Wilson uttered only one word during the court proceedings in Waltham District Court, saying "Yes" when Judge Kevin Doyle asked him if he understood that he had a right to legal counsel. Doyle entered a plea of not guilty on behalf of the defendant.

Wilson underwent a preliminary examination by court psychiatrist Robert Weiner before Doyle continued the case until Aug. 28.

Davee had spent 18 years of her life in and out of mental institutions in Massachusetts and Maine, and was frequently admitted to Metropolitan State Hospital.

On Aug. 9, 1978, according to investigators, Davee was granted a pass which allowed her to walk around the Metropolitan State Hospital grounds without an escort. The pass was authorized by the ward physician, upon recommendation of her treatment team. When she failed to return to her ward that afternoon, the doctor in duty contacted her mother, the director of the hospital unit, and State and Waltham police.

Staff members searching the hospital grounds the following day discovered a hut containing clothes and bed linen. Within 24 hours, the hut was dismantled and the linen sent to the laundry.

Those actions later led to charges that the hospital tried to destroy evidence in the case.

Sen. Jack Backman (D-Brookline), who is chairman of a Senate committee to investigate treatment of patients in state facilities, complained that "the Mental Health Department was not relieved of its responsibility to investigate further, although the matter had been turned over to state and local police.

"By destroying the hut n the hospital grounds, mental health officials concealed evidence in this case," he said.

On Oct. 6, during another search for the missing patient, hospital staff members found a woman's skirt, pieces of cloth, a pocketbook, and small zippered case tied together in a bundle. The pocketbook, identified as Davee's, contained sunglasses, a hatchet and photographs. On the back of the photos were notes written to her.

Last year, Backman investigated the case and learned that seven human teeth had been found among Wilson's possessions on Nov. 13, 1978

It took eight months of intensive investigation by the Attorney General's office to obtain the evidence needed to bring the charges against Wilson, Assistant Atty. Gen. Robert Bohn said yesterday.

Boston Globe Archives
August 15, 1980
Edward Quill

Some crucial pieces of evidence are missing in the case of a man charged with murdering a fellow patent at the Metropolitan State Hospital, Waltham two years ago, according to a state senator who investigated the case.

The defendant in the case, Melvin W. Wilson, 57, is now undergoing 16 days of psychiatric observation at Bridgewater State Hospital to determine if he is competent to stand trial.

Psychiatrists will also try to determine if Wilson was criminally responsible for the slaying of Ann Marie Davee, 36, whose dismembered body was found Tuesday in three shallow graves on a wooden slope on the state hospital's grounds.

Wilson let members of the attorney general's office to the gravesites on Tuesday. Police say the murder took place "on or about Aug. 9, 1978," when both Wilson and Davee were patients at the hospital. Wilson has been a patient of state institutions for about 39 years. His case has been continued to Aug. 28.

However, according to state Sen. Jack Backman (D-Brookline), chairman of a Senate committee which investigated the case last year, significant material evidence in the case appears to be missing. The attorney general's office isn't saying if it has the evidence.

One of the pieces of evidence is a hatchet, possible one of the weapons allegedly used to murder Davee.

Neither the Department of Mental Health (DMH) nor the attorney general's office would comment yesterday on the whereabouts of the hatchet and other items found on the state hospital grounds more than a year and a half ago.

However, Backman said yesterday, "The discovery of the remains of Ann Davee confirms the findings of the Senate Committee to investigate seclusion, restraint and deaths in state-supported facilities. Our review of this case demonstrated utter neglect by the Department of Mental Health in the investigation of Ann Davee's disappearance.

"Nearly two months elapsed before a serious search was conducted. Potential evidence was destroyed. Leads were not followed. The DMH even ignored the discovery of seven of Ms. Davee's teeth, which the Tufts forensic laboratory disclosed were probably extracted after her death."

Backman charged that on Aug. 10, 1978, the day following Davee's disappearance, hospital employees searching the hospital grounds discovered a hut, containing clothes and bed linen, where Davee and Wilson had apparently met. The hut was dismantled within 24 hours and the linen sent to the laundry, Backman said.

During another search for Davee, on Oct. 6, 1978, the hospital staff found a woman's skirt, pieces of cloth, a pocketbook, and a small zippered case, all tied together in a bundle. The pocketbook contained sunglasses, a hatchet, and photographs.

Backman says although he has talked with members from the attorney general's office who investigated the case, he still has not been able to learn the whereabouts of these articles.

Ken Wayne of the attorney general's office said Asst. Gen. Frederick Riley, who conducted the investigation and accompanied Wilson to the gravesites, would have no comment on the matter. Wayne said that any comment on the case would be "inappropriate" at this time.

DMH spokesperson Brooke Pope said, "Sen. Backman's charges put us in a very difficult position to balance the story, because the police have put a lid on this one. They've asked up not to talk about the case."

The Davee case was one of 19 documented cases of death and/or disappearances of persons living in state-supported facilities, all listed in the Backman committee's report published last month/.

Before the discovery of Davee's body, Backman said DMH had listed her as "discharged on Feb. 9,"six months after her disappearance.

"The whole matter is indicative of the way the Department of Mental Health operated," Backman said yesterday. "If you call today you'll get one

answer. In two weeks you'll get another answer. No one is apparently responsible.

"The Davee woman's mother told the committee she was concerned about her daughter's disappearance, that she believed her daughter had been attacked a year before her disappearance. But she told us she got no help form the Mental Health Department."

Following its study, the committee recommended an investigation of DMH, but the bill was vetoed by Gov. Edward J. King, Backman said.

Boston Globe Archives
October 30, 1980

A murder indictment was returned yesterday by the Suffolk County grand jury against Melvin W. Wilson, 57, a former patient at Waltham State Hospital, charging him with killing and dismembering a woman patient there two years ago. Wilson is charged with the slaying of Ann Marie Davee, 36, while they were both patients. Investigator from the office of the Atty. Gen. Francis X. Bellotti entered the case early this year after police allegedly discovered seven human teeth among Wilson's possessions. Davee has been missing since August 9, 1978.

Metropolitan State Hospital became vastly known as the "hospital of the seven teeth." Even today, paranormal teams take the risk of breaking and entering the building in an attempt to get the evidence of a haunting associated with the brutal murder and poor conditions that took place there. Not only the death of Anne Marie Davee, but of untold others who died within the walls of the old hospital.

I talked to the Sheriff who keeps watch over the old hospital. He told me that, on more than one occasion, they had been called out to the old hospital on the report of an apparent suicide. These suicides are most often discovered by paranormal teams who sneak in. What caught my attention more than anything, though, was all the suicides have been found in the exact same spot. Also notable is the fact that all of the victims have been female and all close to the same age range.

In the paranormal field, we often run across circumstances where a pattern much like this will repeat itself throughout the years. Some believe it is the energy within the building itself, drawing on the tragic murder that took place in the old asylum, still remaining there today.

~ CHAPTER SEVEN ~

~ The Real Texas Chainsaw House ~
Plainfield, Wisconsin

The True Story Behind the Texas Chainsaw Massacre

The real house was not in Texas, but in Plainfield, Wisconsin, the home of Ed Gein.

The setting is a secluded farm house Ed once lived in with his mother, father, and brother, Henry. After the death of his mother and father, a fire took the life of his brother. Public records from the time indicate the fire was suspected arson.

In November, 1957, a woman named Bernice Worden, a local store-keeper, went missing. Ed was the last one reported to have been seen with her. When the police arrived at Ed's house to question him, he was not home. The officers decided to take a look around in an out-building. As they entered the out-building, a foul odor permeated through the air, overtaking them. Through the darkness, one of the officers noticed what he thought was a deer carcass, hanging from the rafters. As they approached it, they were

Figure 72. Older picture of Ed Gein house.

Figure 73. More recent photo of Ed Gein house.

sickened by the sight revealed in the beam of their flashlights.

They had stumbled on the gruesome remains of, not a deer, but a human corpse. The corpse had been decapitated and was slit from the groin all the way up to the neck. The police could tell it was what remained of a woman. Beneath is the real photo of the corpse found that day.

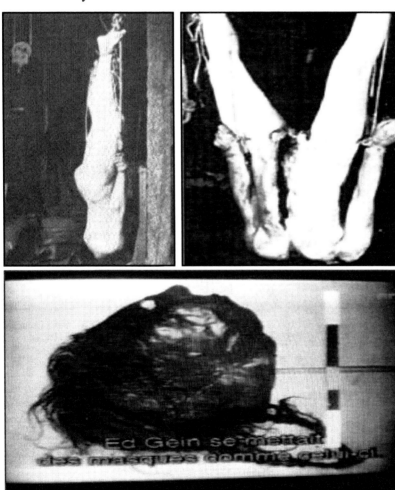

Figures 74, 75 & 76. The pictures above show the gruesomeness of what the police had found upon entering the property of Ed Gein. The scalp of one of his female victims.

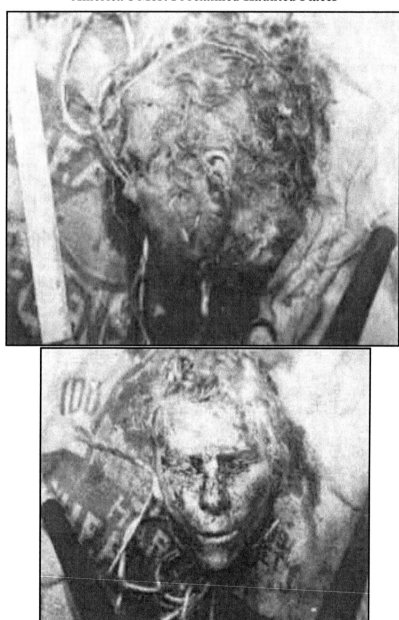

Figures 77 & 78. The head of the missing shop keeper, found in a box inside the house.

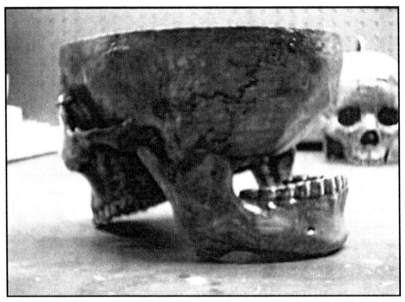

Figure 79. Ed even made things from the skulls of his victims, such as this bowl. Is it the same one he ate his cereal out of?

Figure 80. Photo of Ed Gein.

The police taped off Ed's house and only a short time later arrested Ed Gein. At the police station, Ed told a story that took the police by surprise. Ed Gein stated he was making a suit from female remains, as he was really a woman trapped in a man's body.

<u>Profile</u>

AKA - The Butcher of Plainfield, The Plainfield Butcher, The
 Mad Butcher, The Plainfield Ghoul
DOB/DOD: 1906 - 26 July 1984
Family:{Mother} Augusta 1878-1945
{Father} George 1873-1940
{Brother} Henry 1901-1944
Residence (at Time of Murders): 160-acre farm, seven miles
 outside Plainfield, Wisconsin, USA
Murder Type/Practices - Serial Killer/Grave robbery, Sadism,
 Necrophilia, Cannibalism, Death Fetishism
Method/Weapons Used: Shooting / .22, .32
Organization: Mixed
Mobility: Stable
Victim Vicinity: Plainfield, Wisconsin
Murder Time Span: 1954 - 1957
Victim Type: Old Women
Victims: Mary Hogan (Died 8 Dec 1954), Bernice Worden
 (Died 16 Nov 1957) (+?)

During the trial, Ed was found incompetent to stand trial and ordered confined to a mental hospital. In 1968, Ed Gein finally found himself on trial. However, due to his stretch in the mental hospital, Ed was found not guilty by reason of insanity. He would spend the rest of his life in Mendota State Hospital.

Figure 81. Photo of Mendota State Hospital.

Figure 82. Photo of Mendota State Hospital.

Figure 83. Photo of Mendota State Hospital.

Even after his death, it seemed that victims would still show up. In 1999, in a well on what once was Ed Gein's property, the remains of 6 women and one man were found. When the police were called out, they would neither confirm nor deny whether the bodies were from the time of Ed's killing spree. The remains were taken to the coroner's office but no word was ever heard about it.

Some who live within the town claim to have seen a woman walking on the Gein property. There have even been some who have filed police reports. Due to the burning of the house and his property, I do not know of any paranormal team which has evidence to support any of the claims to the sightings and reports of the paranormal activity alleged to take place on the prior Ed Gein property.

~ CHAPTER EIGHT ~

~ Villisca Axe Murder House ~
Villisca, Iowa

The True Story Behind the J.B. Moore House Axe Murders

In the early 1900's a small town by the name of Villisca in Iowa would become known as one of the most famous unsolved murder houses. Villisca was a quiet town where everyone knew everyone. The Main Street was lined with quaint, little stores. Several times a day trains would pull in and out of the relatively busy Train Depot. But, on June 10th, 1912, the town of Villisca, Iowa, would be changed forever. It was in the early morning hours of June 10th, the Moore family lay sleeping in their beds. Also two overnight guests of the Moore children, Lena Stillinger (age twelve) and her sister, Ina Stillinger (age eight), were sleeping in the downstairs bedroom just off the front parlor. In the still of that fateful night, an incident occurred that shook the very foundation of the quiet little town to its core.

The Moore family was well known and much loved by every

Figure 84. Early photo of the Moore house.

one in Villisca. In the darkness of the night, a figure moved silently throughout the house, carrying an axe that they brought in from outside of the Moore's quiet, simple home. As dawn set in around five a.m., a neighbor named Mary Peckham was out hanging her daily laundry. She noticed it was a bit unusual not to see Sarah Moore out tending to her daily chores, as well.

Sarah's normal routine was much like Mary's. The fact that Sarah had not been seen yet was a bit odd. As the morning continued, Mary began to notice no one came out of her neighbors' house all morning. In fact, an eerie silence hung over the little house next door. As concern overwhelmed her, she walked next door and knocked on the door of the Moore's house. There was no answer. After she let their chickens out, Mary returned to her house and placed a call to Josiah's Moore's brother, Ross Moore.

Shortly after nine a.m., Ross arrived at his brother's house. He

Figure 85. Current photo of what is now The Villisca Axe Murder House.

walked around the side of the house and peered in through the window. Unable to see anything through the darkened windows, he retuned to the front porch and pulled out his spare key. As he opened the door, the house had an uneasy, eerie silence to it.

Ross Moore, brother to Josiah Moore, brother in law to Sarah Moore, and uncle to their three children, entered the bedroom off the parlor. He was met with a gruesome sight. He first found the bodies of the Stillinger girls, bludgeoned to death where they lay sleeping only hours earlier. The two girls who spent the night with the Moore family had been brutally and savagely murdered as had the rest of the household. Staggering out the door, Ross called to Mary to get the City Marshall.

A short time later Hank Horton, Villisca's City Marshall, arrived at the Moore house. As he climbed the stairs to the bedrooms, he was greeted with a grisly sight that would haunt him

111

Figure 86. An earlier photo of Josiah and Sarah Moore with 2 of their children.

Figure 87. Shown above: Top Row - The Moores Children; Bottom Two - Stillinger Children

for the rest of his days. All 6 members of the Moore family, along with the two innocent little overnight guests, had been brutally murdered.

The Victims

Josiah Moore (age 43)

Sarah Montgomery Moore (age 44)

Herman Moore (age 11)

Katherine Moore (age 9)

Boyd Moore (age 7)

Paul Moore (age 5)

{And, the two overnight guests of Katherine}

Lena Stillinger (age 12)

Ina Stillinger (age 8)

Figure 88. Newspaper headlines in the wake of the grisly murders.

As the town reeled from the news of the grisly murders, a reward was soon offered.

There were a few suspects, of course, that the Marshall and other members of law enforcement were looking into; One suspect being Sarah's brother in law, Lee Van Gilder. He was the ex-husband of Sarah's sister, Mary Van Gilder. Lee van Gilder was well known by the police for his violence and affinity for pornography. He was later cleared. Law enforcement now had four viable, prime suspects. Shown below are the suspects in question at that time.

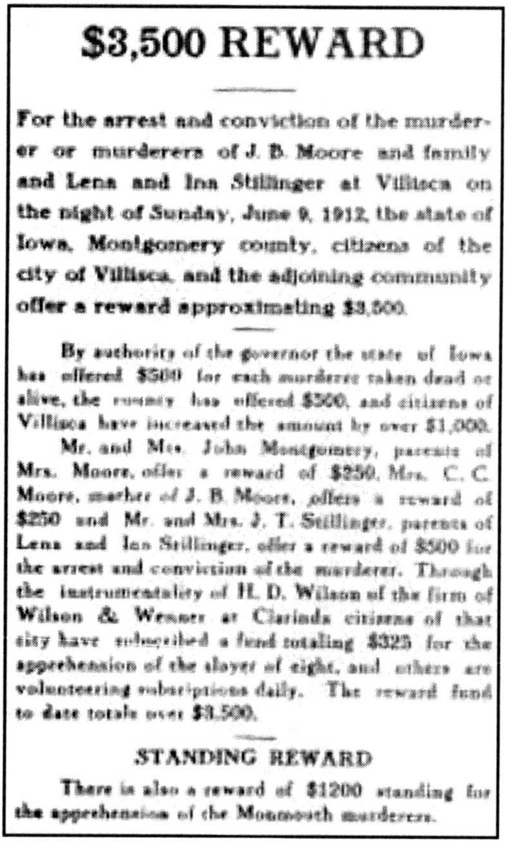

$3,500 REWARD

For the arrest and conviction of the murderer or murderers of J. B. Moore and family and Lena and Ina Stillinger at Villisca on the night of Sunday, June 9, 1912, the state of Iowa, Montgomery county, citizens of the city of Villisca, and the adjoining community offer a reward approximating $3,500.

By authority of the governor the state of Iowa has offered $500 for each murderer taken dead or alive, the county has offered $500, and citizens of Villisca have increased the amount by over $1,000. Mr. and Mrs. John Montgomery, parents of Mrs. Moore, offer a reward of $250, Mrs. C. C. Moore, mother of J. B. Moore, offers a reward of $250 and Mr. and Mrs. J. T. Stillinger, parents of Lena and Ina Stillinger, offer a reward of $500 for the arrest and conviction of the murderer. Through the instrumentality of H. D. Wilson of the firm of Wilson & Wesner at Clarinda citizens of that city have subscribed a fund totaling $325 for the apprehension of the slayer of eight, and others are volunteering subscriptions daily. The reward fund to date totals over $3,500.

STANDING REWARD

There is also a reward of $1200 standing for the apprehension of the Monmouth murderers.

Figure 89. Bulletin showing the reward that was offered in the days after the murders.

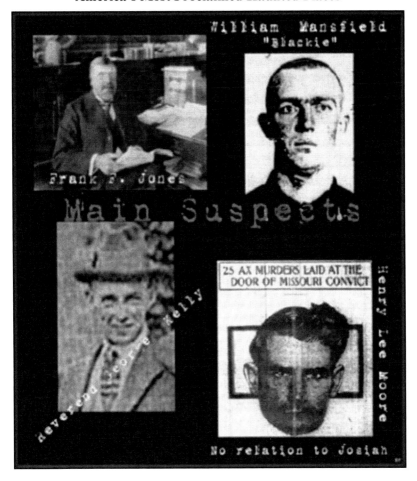

Figure 90. Photo collage showing the various murder suspects.

One of the prime suspects in the Moore murders was Reverend Lyn George Jacklin Kelly, who was a traveling minister and a known "peeping tom". Jacklin Kelly attended the children's day services at the Moore's church on the night of the murders. Early morning about five-thirty a.m., Kelly boarded a train and sat next to an elderly couple on the same train. The elderly couple reported that Kelly told them about the murders before the bodies were ever found. It was years later when Kelly confessed to the murders, but then, right before the trial, he retracted the statement. He stood trial twice for the 8 brutal axe murders. At the first trial, the charges were dropped. During the second trial, the police brought the charges against him once again, but this time a jury acquitted him.

The next suspect was a man by the name of Henry Lee Moore. He was in no way related to the victims. Henry was a drifter prone to outbreaks of violence. He was prosecuted in December of 1912, for the brutal murder of his mother and grandmother with an axe. But it was the eighteen months of brutal slayings over five states of twenty people that would shed some light on what kind of killer he truly was. Unable to make any headway in the case, the Villisca Marshall asked the federal authorities to help them. A man named M.W. McClaughry was assigned to the case.

When McClaughry walked into the crime scene, it was all too familiar a sight. The brutal axe murders and the crime scene left in its wake were almost identical to the ones he saw in a number of states. In 1911, six victims , a family named Wayne, were murdered in Colorado Springs. There were also the murders of the Dewson family in Illinois and another group of mass axe murders included the Showman family in Kansas. There were many others in addition to these. McClaughry was convinced the murders in Villisca were by the same killer they called the "Transient Maniac." He felt certain the murders were committed by Henry Moore. Moore was already serving a life sentence and was, allegedly, seen in Villisca only days before the murders.

After seeing many of the documents of this case, it seems to me that Henry Moore would be the most likely to have committed the murders. His "m.o." shows up over and over again. However, there is one thing missing from the Villisca house murders classic to the rest of the murders. At the scene of the other murders committed by

Moore, the crime scenes were clean with no murder weapon found. This deviates from the evidence at the Moore home. In this scene, the mess was substantial and the axe was left behind. In fact, Moore reportedly only used his father's axe. The axe used in the crime in question, was actually from the home of the Moore's, themselves. Serial killers do not deviate from their set pattern of behavior. The axe in question was Henry Moore's calling card, so to speak.

The next suspect was William Mansfield, aka "Blackie". William was quickly dismissed as the killer after it was proven he

Figure 91. Known portrait of William "Blackie" Mansfield.

was in Illinois at the time of the murders, and that, in fact, he had never been to Villisca.

Senator Frank Jones, the state senator at the time, was at one time J.B. Moore's boss. Until 1908, when J. B. Moore quit to open his own shop, taking with him the most lucrative account Frank Jones had, the John Deere Franchise. Adding insult to injury was the local gossip that J.B. Moore was having an affair with Frank's daughter in-law, Donna. This caused Frank's son, Albert, to lose all composure. He flew into a fit of rage. But, as fate would have it, Albert Jones was never considered a suspect. It was documented that the police were never allowed to talk to Albert since his Father was a local politician with much political clout and many powerful friends. Frank Jones was able to prevent the police ever having access to his son for questioning.

At the time of the Kelly trial, one reporter was said to have overheard Jones and his son, Albert discussing their fear of a witness. That witness could place Albert entering the house of the Moore family, on the night of the murders. Several days following his release of this information, the reporter was murdered. Was he murdered for uncovering the truth about the horrible potential copycat axe murders? Here is a clipping from a newspaper article at that time, discussing the death.

Noel Killed In Villisca Feud?
Omaha, Neb., Nov. 3, 1917

Detective L.W. Longneck is inclined to believe that J.W. Noel, Villisca photographer, who was found dead at Albia, Ia. Thursday with a bullet hole in his forehead, was murdered. He had no definite theory to offer, but bases his opinion on the tense feeling in Montgomery county. "My only surprise is that there has not been a killing before this. I would not be surprised to hear of other shootings before this affair is cleared up" he said. "Noel," he continued, "testified at the Jones-Wilkerson slander suit a year ago that he overheard a conversation in

Jones' machine shop in Villisca. There was supposed to have been a crack in the boards through which he claimed to have heard a conversation between Senator F.F. Jones and his son, Albert. Noel claimed the information he overheard indicated that Jones and his son were afraid of Ed Landers. At the recent Kelly trial, you will recall, Landers testified that on the evening of the murder he observed Albert Jones enter the Moore home at about [illegible] o'clock. His testimony was impeached by the prosecution. Noel and Landers were boon companions." Noel was star witness in the Jones slander suit against Detective J.N. Wilkerson, and one of the strongest supporters of Wilkerson in his fight in Montgomery county, Iowa, to bring about the acquittal of Rev. Lyn G.J. Kelly for the Villisca axe murders.

Even today, the murders at the Villisca house remain unsolved. After 98 years, they are no closer to solving the murders, than they where back in 1912. The fact remains the killer took his confession to his grave. I had the chance to talk to the owner of the Villisca Axe Murder House, a kind, gentle man, Darwin Linn, who takes care of his ill and bed-ridden sister. When I asked him, "If there was one thing you would want in this book about your house, what would it be?" His answer took me by surprise. He simply told me he "wanted to know who the killer truly was."

His story was one I had yet to hear in my six years of researching historically haunted places. Darwin told me, he bought the house to restore the history to it and had done ninety percent of the work himself. He even bought an old barn from the 1912 time period then moved it to the land using his Toyota pick up. Mr. Darwin Linn was a farmer.

When he bought the old house, his wife, Martha, told him they would never be able to rent the old house because of the tragic history associated with it. Darwin answered simply, "I have not bought it to rent it out, I have bought it to keep history alive. In all my years of research, I have only found two places where the owners are not all about the money. They have a real love for their town and strive to preserve the history of it. One is the Villisca Axe Murder House and the other is the Pride. It is people like them who make me want to put out another book. *Thank you, guys.*

~ CHAPTER NINE ~

~ The Bird-Cage Theater ~
Tombstone, Arizona

Tombstone was founded in 1877 by a prospector named Ed Schieffelin. At the time Schieffelin was staying at a place called Camp Huachuca. Ed loved the wilderness, often venturing off alone to look for rocks, even though he had been warned by the soldiers of the dangers. The soldiers often told him the only stone he was going to find out in that vast, desert land was his own tombstone.

But Ed did find his stone, it was sliver. With the words of the soldiers echoing in the back of his mind, he decided to name his first mine, "Tombstone". Soon the word of Ed's silver strike spread. Prospectors from all over descended on the land in hopes of striking it rich. In 1879, another site was laid out on the nearest level spot to the mine shaft for the purpose of appeasing all the prospectors who came to set up homesteads. It was known as "Goose Flats" and was eventually renamed "Tombstone" after the mine.

In the mid 1880's, Tombstone's population grew to 7,500

Figure 92. Photo of Ed Schieffelin.

people on record. This excluded women and children along with any others who lived in the town under the age of twenty-one. The towns' actual population would actually have been closer to 10,000 to 11,000 people total.

Tombstone was one of the fastest growing towns. Home to over one hundred saloons, numerous restaurants and a large red light district, the most famous of all was the Bird-Cage Theater. The Bird-Cage was not just a saloon, but a theater, a gambling hall, and a brothel all in one. A place most of the proper women and men of the town passed by from the opposite side of the street rather than be seen walking in front.

The bird-cage opened on Christmas day in 1881, never to close its doors on any day of the week for entire time it operated. The Bird-Cage was aptly named for the rooms where the ladies of the night entertained their guests. The photo below is the old Bird-Cage the way it is today.

The most violent of murders that took place within the walls of the Bird-Cage was the murder of Margarita, a prostitute. One night she sat on the lap of a well known gambler, Billy Milgreen, known to be the best customer of "Gold Dollar", another prostitute from a rival establishment known as the Crystal Palace. Allegedly, Gold Dollar and Margarita argued only days before. Gold Dollar told her to stay away from Billy Milgreen or she would cut her heart out. One of Gold Dollar's friends who worked at the Bird-Cage told Gold Dollar about Margarita sitting on Billy's lap, flirting, and making moves on him. Infuriated, Gold Dollar went to the Bird-Cage. As Gold Dollar saw Margarita sitting on his lap, she flew into a fit of rage. She grabbed her stiletto knife and plunged it into Margarita's chest, attempting to cut her heart out. Just then, the town marshal walked in. Gold Dollar ran out back hiding the knife, knowing that without a weapon they could not get her for murder.

The Bird-Cage became well known for the men who visited

Figure 93. Tombstone in the early days.

there. Doc Holliday was often seen at the Bird-Cage along with Wyatt Earp.

It was at the Bird-Cage where Wyatt Earp, a well known lawman, had his affair with one of the women who worked there. That woman, Sarah Marcus, would later become his wife. It was even speculated, at one time, that the OK Corral gunfight was over Sarah.

There were an estimated sixteen gun and/or knife fights which took place within the walls of the Bird-Cage leaving behind twenty-six dead before it closed its doors forever in 1889. There still remains an estimated one hundred forty-four bullet holes within the walls and flooring of the old Bird Cage. These serve as a reminder of just how wild the Old West truly was.

The Bird-Cage Theater is known today as one of the most popular paranormal hot spots. Many of the women who go to the

Figure 94. Old photo of the main street in Tombstone.

Figure 95. Undated photo of The Bird-Cage Theater in Tombstone.

Figure 96. The curtains are even the same ones from the operational days of the bird cage, dating back to the late1800's.

Figure 97. Interior view of The Bird-Cage Theater in Tombstone.

Bird-Cage report having their butt slapped or pinched. Even those who don't believe in the paranormal, soon find themselves a believer.

Ghosts of the old Bird-Cage Theater

Possibly one of the most reported spirits at the Bird-Cage is the old stage-hand. The stage-hand was a man by the name of Richard. He is often seen near the stage area, as what some classify as a shadow person. I have spoken to many paranormal teams and all have had the same sighting of this tall, shadow figure on or around the stage.

Next, is a woman who is suspected to have worked at the Bird-Cage in its later years. Thought to be a woman named Cassie, she was a seventeen year old prostitute. It is said that many have seen

Figure 98. (Left) Photo of Wyatt Earp.

Figure 99. (Right) Photo of Doc Holliday.

Figure 100. (Left) Photo of Sarah Marcus.

Figure 101. Sarah Marcus' {aka Josephine} bordello room.

her and have caught her on EVPs. I have found no historical records of her anywhere in the archives or on the internet, but that does not mean she was not there. It seems a lot was lost during two fires that consumed the town of Tombstone, taking with them a lot of the documents and historical records. Despite this, though, much of the history still lives on today in the town of Tombstone. It was a town that refused to die; A town that remains inhabited by those who lived there long, long ago.

~ CHAPTER TEN ~

~ Sloss Furnace ~
Birmingham, Alabama

Colonel James Withers Sloss was one of the founding fathers of Birmingham, Alabama. A man well known for helping in the progression of railroad development in Birmingham, he is also attributed to participating in the upbringing of the Coke and Coal Company in the 1800's. Sloss came to open his own company after his enrollment with the Coke and Coal Company. Naming his new company, Sloss Furnace, he built a company to bring metals up from the ground using blasting from dynamite. The company sits on 50 acres given to him by the Elyton Land Company for industrial development.

James Sloss brought in Harry Hargreaves, a former student of the English inventor, Thomas Whitwell, as the head engineer in charge of construction. The first blast took place in April of 1882. Within the first year of it being open, 24,000 tons of quality iron was produced. In 1886, James Sloss retired, selling the company to a group of investors who changed the name in 1899 to Sloss-

Figure 102. Old undated drawing of the Sloss Furnace.

Figure 103. Undated photo of the Sloss Furnace.

Figure 104. Undated photo of Colonel James Withers Sloss.

Sheffield Steel and Iron Company. During that time, the company built 48 small cabins for the black workers.

In the 1880's, the plant grew and so did the number of men working there.

With the war, there was a call for more steel and the prisons signed with the mining company to lease convicts for nine dollars a month. In 1910 Sloss–Sheffield built a prison of their own so the convicts would be close by.

Most of the convicts, it was reported, never saw the daylight as they were down in the mines all day. It is said in the time it was open there were near sixty deaths. As I began to research further, I spent a lot of time looking into this. I came across some old newspapers that talked about some of the deaths at Sloss.

One story, in particular, caught my attention. It was the story of a man who had fallen into a vat of smoldering iron, leaving only a foot and shoe behind. In September of 1887, it was said, a man lost his footing and fell to his death into the smelting iron. I, being a stickler for details, took some time and looked it up. According to some of the records, there was a death in 1887 where a man named Richard, aka Theophilus Calvin, did in fact die while working at Sloss. He was changing a machine belt and fell in. This is also documented by the death certificate.

Figure 105. One of the quarters built for black workers.

Figure 106. The inside of one of the old Sloss quarters.

America's Most Proclaimed Haunted Places

Figure 107. Photo of the prison.

Figure 108. Photo of some of the mine workers.

133

Figures 109 & 110. Above and below are some photos from inside Sloss Furnace.

America's Most Proclaimed Haunted Places

Below are only some of the deaths that made the papers.

"Three Men Killed" <u>Birmingham Age-Herald</u> 8 Jan 1895: 5. (2 killed at Sloss;

"Heavy Damage Suit Filed Against the Sloss Iron & Steel Company Yesterday for Death of F. W. Hartman: Deceased was Killed While Confined in the Mines as a Convict, Sent Up from the Police Court" <u>Birmingham Age-Herald</u> 23 March 1898: 5.

"Negro Miner Killed" <u>Birmingham News</u> 13 Sep 1899: 3. (Tom Evans)

"Convict Fell 150 Feet" <u>Birmingham News</u> 28 Sep 1899: p. 7 (Henry Reed)

"A Fatal Affray: Colored [sic] Miner Killed" <u>Birmingham News</u> 7 Oct 1899: 2. (Frank Derricot)

"Five are Killed and 35 Injured in Mine Accident: Cars Run Wild in Sloss Slope No. 1, Plunging Miners to Bottom" 12 July 1923: <u>Birmingham News</u> 12 July 1923: 1, 13. (includes list of dead)

"Five Negro Miners Killed, 29 Injured: Fatal Accident in Sloss Mine at Bessemer" <u>Birmingham Post</u> 12 July 1923: 1, 7. (includes names of dead, fatally injured, seriously injured, and badly injured)

"Eight is Toll in Accident in Ore Mine: Four Negroes Instantly Killed, Three Others Die During Day, Another During Night; Coupling Breaks" <u>Birmingham Age-Herald</u> 13 July 1923: 1, 2. (Includes list of casualties)

"Deaths in Mine Crash Number 8: Remainder of Injured are Expected to Live; 15 Still in Hospital" <u>Birmingham News</u> 13 July 1923: 19.

"Toll of Mine Dead is Eight: 26 Remaining Injured are Reported Improving" <u>Birmingham Post</u> 13 July 1923: 1.

"5 Killed, 35 Hurt in Mine: Train of Trip Cars Breaks in Alabama Shaft, Plunging 800 Feet" <u>New York Times</u> 13 July 1923.

America's Most Proclaimed Haunted Places

It is said to this day, the ones who go into these places often have the feeling of being watched and many times voices are heard when no one is around to speak. This is indeed one of the only places that, as I heard the stories behind the haunting, I was able to find death records to corroborate the stories I had been told. The only one I have not been able to verify is a report that a young girl committed suicide.

The story goes that in the early 1920's, a young girl discovered she was pregnant and committed suicide on the grounds of the old factory. Now, there are two problems with this story. First, at that time, no women were allowed on the plant property. Second, there are no records to back this up. There are records backing up a few murders, but it was during the time when the prison was operational there. There was never a record of anyone being murdered in the mines.

Sloss Furnace is reportedly haunted by the ghost of an extremely angry and pushy shift foreman, nicknamed Slagg. Legend has it this foreman was particularly hard on the men and was allegedly responsible for several deaths. Although there were several murders, guilt has never been unequivocally proven. It is unreasonable to assume the man who died in the vat was pushed, as legend and lore allude. Activity is reportedly high, and extremely unfriendly on the grounds of the old factory. The conditions are dangerous, rusty, and treacherous. Caution should be used by any who go there seeking to antagonize the unfriendly spirits of its past.

My partner in this venture had the opportunity to investigate here, at Sloss Furnace. In Feb of 2009, she and several other paranormal investigators investigated with Patrick Burns, as well as with Dave and Tom of Para-X Radio. I have included a statement and some photographs from her:

America's Most Proclaimed Haunted Places

I had heard the rumors that Sloss could be a dangerous place to hunt. The entities were indeed negative there, and throughout the night several people were attacked. I was one of those people. We had encountered a negative entity under the boiler room. At the exact same time that my Mel-Meter registered a 200mg spike, I felt a hot, searing pain on my leg. I was wearing high laced combat boots, and was unable to really investigate the pain until I was back in our hotel room several hours later. Upon removing my combat boots, in front of several witnesses, it was discovered that there was a large, pronounced bite mark in the location where I had felt the pain earlier that night. Also that night, I was changing the batteries in my camera during a ghost box session. At the moment the batteries were removed from my camera, we all heard a loud growl. Suddenly, there was a whoosh!, followed by a burst of air, and then a loud "POP", that sounded like a gun shot. Sparks flew out of my hands, and my camera, with no batteries in it, had exploded in my hands. That was the end of a very uncomfortable night of investigation for me .~ T. Fontaine Feb. 2009

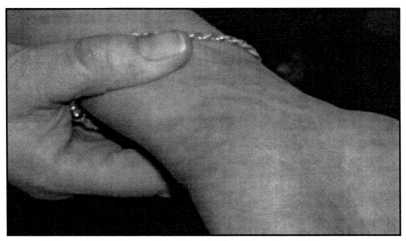

Figure 111. The burn on the palm of her hand from the exploding camera

137

~ CHAPTER ELEVEN ~

~Moundsville Penitentiary~
Moundsville, WV

Moundsville Penitentiary, better known by its given name, West Virginia Penitentiary, was built in 1876. It was a small prison and would fast become over crowded. In 1929, the prison was expanded to accommodate its ever growing prisoner population. During the time the penitentiary was open, ninety-four men were executed in the gallows. The town's people would, on the day of an execution, pack a picnic lunch and head to the hills just outside of the prison, which gave a clear view of the Hangman's Gallows, allowing them to watch as the men were hung. The executions at Moundsville were all well documented. The following is a list of men and dates who were executed in the penitentiary:

EXECUTIONS (1899-1914)

»Sheep Caldwell (n/a)
»Frank Broaden ax (Nov. 9, 1899)
»Frank Walker (Dec. 15, 1899)
»George Carter (Mar. 21, 1902)

»Louis Young (May 1, 1902)
»John Mooney (May 9, 1902)
»Frank Friday (May 9, 1902)
»Perry Christian (Jun. 13, 1902)
»State Henry (Oct. 24, 1902)
»Wilfred Davis (Jun. 5, 1903)

America's Most Proclaimed Haunted Places

Figure 112. Exterior image of the Moundsville Penitentiary.

»George Williams (Sept. 9, 1904)
»Frank Johnson (Jul. 17, 1908)
»Authur Brown (Aug. 20, 1909)
»Thomas Wayne (Dec. 23, 1910)
»Jesse Cook (Feb. 10, 1911)
»Frank Stephenson (Feb. 17, 1911)
»William Furbish (Mar. 17, 1911)
»James Williams (Apr. 4, 1913)
»John Marshall (Apr. 4, 1913)
»Henry Sterling (Apr. 11, 1913)
»John Hix (Jun. 6, 1913)
»Henry Green (Mar. 6, 1914)
»Silas Jones (Jul. 10, 1914)

EXECUTIONS (1927-1937)

»Pierce Jeffries (Feb. 18, 1927)
»Wesley Swain (Feb. 3, 1928)
»Andrew Brady (Mar. 30, 1928)
»Lawrence Fike (Aug. 10, 1928)

»Henry Brogan (Feb. 8, 1929)
»Theodore Carr (Jun. 14, 1929)
»Millard Morrison (Sept. 13, 1929)
»Walter Wilmoy (Sept. 13, 1929)
»Walter Crabtree (May 9, 1930)
»Roosevelt Darnell (Nov. 14, 1930)
»Emory Stephens (Feb. 20, 1931)
»Will Adams (Feb. 20, 1931)
»Frank Hyer (Jun. 19, 1931)
»Harry Powers (Mar. 18, 1932)
»James Blount (May 12, 1932)
»Omer Brill (Aug. 10, 1933)
»Leo Fraser (Nov. 24, 1933)
»Joe Corey (Dec. 8, 1933)
»Greely Blankenship (Jan. 7, 1935)
»Robert Branch (Jan. 19, 1935)
»Frank Pramesa (Apr. 13, 1937)
»Willie Beckner (Jun. 25, 1937)
»Marvin Brown (Sept. 10, 1937)
»William

America's Most Proclaimed Haunted Places

EXECUTIONS (1938-1959)

»Styres Raymond (Mar. 13, 1938)
»Arnett Booth (Mar. 21, 1938)
»John Travis (Mar. 21, 1938)
»Orville Adkins (Mar. 21, 1938)
»Bysantine Hartman (Jun. 28, 1940)
»Paul Tross (Dec. 6, 1940)
»James Chambers (Mar. 30, 1945)
»William Turner (Dec. 28, 1945)
»Richard Collins (Oct. 11, 1946)
»William Gorden (Jan. 3, 1947)
»Paul Burton (Jan. 2, 1948)
»Mark McCauley (Jan. 30, 1948)
»Mathew O. Perison (Sept. 23, 1948)
»Lemuel Steed (Oct. 15, 1948)
»Bud Peterson (Feb. 25, 1949)
»Fred Painter (Mar. 26, 1951)
»Harry Burdette (Mar. 26, 1951)
»James Hewlett (Apr. 10, 1951)
»Oshel Gardner (Apr. 17, 1953)

»Tom Ingram (Mar. 27, 1954)
»Robert Hopkins (Sept. 7, 1956)
»Eugene Linger (Jun. 5, 1958)
»Larry Fudge (Jul. 1, 1958)
»Elmer Brunner (Apr. 3, 1959)

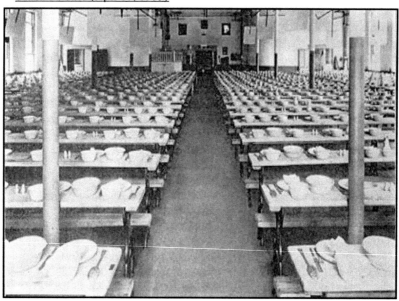

Figure 113. Undated image of the mess hall within the penitentiary.

140

America's Most Proclaimed Haunted Places

Below is the press release and public statement issued about the first of the riots:

Moundsville Prisoners Riot; Holding 5 Guards Hostage

Wheeling News-Register
March 20, 1973

At least two convicts were hospitalized and five guards at the West Virginia Penitentiary at Moundsville were being held hostage during a full-scale riot that broke out at the prison this morning.

There was a report from the prison shortly after noon that the rioting convicts threatened to shoot the five hostages if State Police or prison guards fired gunshots or tear gas at them.

A fire in the basement of the prison was reported to be burning out of control at 12:30 pm.

State Police armed with gas masks entered the Penitentiary and were stationed around the outside to block off streets to pedestrian and car traffic.

"They're tearing hell out the place," said Howard Riggs of 2 Kermit Ct., who lives at the southern tip of the Penitentiary.

At 10:30 am the convicts apparently set fire to the Penitentiary as Riggs reported he could see smoke coming from inside the walls. Moundsville City fire trucks were still inside the prison walls at noon but Riggs reported the smoke had subsided by that time.

Two of the three inmates taken to the Reynolds Memorial Hospital were reported suffering from stab wounds. There was no immediate report on their condition.

Penitentiary Warden William O. Wallace confirmed that five guards were being held hostage by the convicts but declined to reveal their identity until their families are notified.

Riggs said the rioting could easily be heard from outside the prison walls. "There was glass breaking and a lot of cussing and hollering. The convicts were hollering obscenities to people outside," Riggs stated.

The first report of what triggered the riot was that a group of convicts overpowered a guard and took his keys to the solitary confinement section of the prison. There they released Bobby Gene Jarvis, the convict who has been indicted and is awaiting trial for the murder last October of prison guard, William Quilliams.

Another report was that a convict identified as Paul Ellis Davis, who has killed two inmates while confined to the Penitentiary, then released 17 other prisoners from confinement and these inmates then triggered the riot and eventually took five guards hostage.

A member of the construction crew, which was ordered away from the Penitentiary when the riot broke out, identified Davis. The construction crew was working on improvements at the prison. Prisoners from the maximum-security section of the prison were demanding to talk with a representative of Gov. Arch A. Moore, Jr.

Wallace said that Moore's special assistant Norman Yost had left Charleston by helicopter at 11:30 am and was expected in Moundsville shortly after noon.

Wallace said that the men have not revealed their

grievance but according to one report the riot began early this morning when a guard was taking a group of prisoners to the bath area and a prisoner identified only as Davis reportedly jumped a guard, and grabbed his keys.

The prisoners barricaded themselves in the maximum-security section of the prison and have threatened to kill the five hostages if any shots or tear-gas are fired into the area.

Tension mounted around the prison as Wallace, the State Police, guards and Marshall County Sheriff's deputies wearing shields and hard hats brandished shotguns and rifles.

Traffic has been cordoned off around the prison, and smoke still poured from a south entrance on Jefferson Avenue at noon.

Spectators outside could see the smashed windows inside the prison.

It was estimated by officials that about 35 "hard-core" convicts were involved in the rioting and taking of the five hostages.

Approximately 170 law enforcement officers - state and local - were on the scene.

Wallace said the inmates in the prison had volunteered to try to extinguish the fire burning out of control in the prison basement, if guards would put a hose inside.

However, one guard said that only old clothing was stored in the burning section, but that it was impossible to determine how bad the fire was getting. At 12:30 pm prisoners began again to break windows in the prison.

After the riot, the prison was kept under tight control. Until, thirteen years later, on January 2nd, when the second riot occurred.

Below is the newspaper clipping from that riot, as well:

W.Va. Pen Inmates Riot; 12 Hostages Being Held

News-Register Staff Writer
January 2, 1986
Bulletin!

Several relatives of those currently being held hostage by inmates at the West Virginia State Penitentiary at Moundsville are demanding to speak with Gov. Arch A. Moore Jr. in what was reported to be an impassioned plea for the safety of loved ones held inside the 100-year-old maximum-security prison.

Speaking to the news media briefly this morning, officials on the scene revealed that one of the hostages, Bill Henderson, a guard, had contacted his wife, Melanie, saying, "That if they (police officials) storm the place, someone will die."

Meanwhile, there has been no official word on the demands the inmates are making for the release of the hostages other than a request to meet with Moore.

Negotiations continued late this morning with inmates at the West Virginia Penitentiary at Moundsville who Wednesday evening gained control of a portion of the state's maximum-security facility.

Twelve persons - 11 corrections officers and one food

service personnel - are being held by a group of inmates.

Two other hostages were released on Wednesday evening and the other this morning.

Although no formal demands have been made by the inmates, three employees - Paul Kirby, who heads the medical division, David Fromhart, a sections chief and Jeff Fromhart, a counselor - have met with the inmates several hours since the 5:30 pm takeover.

The inmates reportedly want to talk with Gov. Arch Moore Jr., who has said through his press secretary John Price that he will not talk with the inmates until the hostages have been released and the institution is returned back to correctional officials.

Moore was in Florida on a vacation at the time of the takeover.

One inmate has died. He was Kent Slie, serving a life term for murder from Putnam County. Slie was born in New Martinsville.

The two hostages released were Mike Coleman and Eddie Littell. Coleman reportedly had suffered chest pains and Littell had an injured arm. Neither was admitted to the hospital.

The hostages have been identified as: Patrick Glascock, Robert Hill, Robert Johnson, Mike Smith, John Wilson, Bill Wright, Robert Jones, Sanford Clegg, Leslie Howearth, Russell Lorentz, Joe Hill (all correctional officers). Bill Henderson, a food service employee, was also taken.

A new food service firm, Serv-A Mation, began operation Wednesday; the former food server had employed Henderson.

America's Most Proclaimed Haunted Places

The inmates, who began their takeover during the supper hour Wednesday, have control of the southern section of the institution. They reportedly broke into the control unit, which houses the most hardened criminals.

In addition to the control unit, the men involved in the siege reside in the New Wall and P. & R. units. The men have access to the dining hall and the infirmary.

Wednesday evening state police from sections of the state were called to the institution, and appeared in riot gear, along with all off-duty correctional officers, Marshall County sheriff's deputies and Moundsville City police.

The inmates seized the prison in a riot inside the dining hall while the evening meal was served.

"We don't want this any more that you do," one inmate yelled out a window. "You quit treating us like dogs, this wouldn't happen."

"We want better living conditions, better facilities and better medical conditions. They treat us just like dogs in here. This ain't going to go on."

State police said between 125 and 200 inmates out of a prison population of about 740 were involved.

Authorities had control of the prison guard towers. Spotlights played on the prison walls and there was the occasional sound of breaking glass. Smoke drifted above the prison walls at times.

More than six hours after the riot broke out, leaders of the rebellion began compiling a list of demands to be presented to the warden over walkie-talkies taken from the captive guards.

There were no reports of injuries and none of the

prison's 742 convicts had escaped, officials said, but 100 police in riot gear ringed the prison to prevent a breakout while a large crowd of townspeople milled about and stood on porches across the street.

Bill Wallace, one of the bystanders outside the prison, said he heard inmates shouting demands out windows for "better medical services, better living quarters, a pizza and some women."

"I feel sorry for the poor people in there but if they didn't do what they did, they wouldn't be in there," Wallace said.

Warden Jerry Hedrick told reporters at an impromptu news conference outside the prison that the takeover started in the dining hall but that the inmates appeared to have abandoned it for two cell blocks in the south end of the facility.

"At this particular time they are going to send a list of demands," Hedrick said. "We will take a look at that but that is all we are doing now."

"They pretty much have the run of the place, right now. Everything is peaceful. I don't know how well organized it is."

The warden said the prisoners had set no deadlines and had made no threats that he was aware of.

He said the inmates did not get any weapons from the guards but added, "of course they manufacture weapons in there."

The prison had "about 30" guards on duty at the time of the takeover, Hedrick said.

Corrections Commissioner A. V. Dodrill rejected demands by riot leaders to meet with Moore.

"They said they would not talk to anyone until they talk to Gov. Moore, but I told the staff he would not be available." Said William Whyte, executive aide to Dodrill.

When the inmates were denied an audience with Moore, some took off their clothes and set them on fire, officials said.

Officials said one of the hostages was an employee of Morrison Food Service, the firm under contract to prepare prison meals. The prison, under orders to make vast reforms, was the scene of a 1973 riot that left one inmate dead and two others wounded. Six years ago, 15 convicts staged a mass escape in which an off-duty sate trooper and one of the fugitives were killed.

The riots brought to light some of the harsh conditions the prisoners were subjected to and living in as the prison fell victim to overcrowding once again. During the time the prison remained open, it was under the operational control of many different and very strict wardens. The list of wardens was extensive.

NAME	SERVED	TITLE
George S. McFadden	1866-1870	Warden
William B. Curtis	1870-1871	Warden
Thomas Paul Shallcross	1871-1873	Warden
William L. Bridges	1873-1881	Warden
Thomas J. West	1881-1885	Warden
John E. Peck	1885-1887	Warden
Edward Robertson	1887-1889	Warden
M. Van Pelt	1889-1897	Warden
Samuel A. Hawk	1897-1901	Warden

America's Most Proclaimed Haunted Places

NAME	SERVED	TITLE
Charles E. Haddox	1901-1908	Warden
C. G. Dawson	1908-1909	Acting Warden
Joseph E. Mathews	1909-1911	Warden
M. L. Brown	1911-1914	Warden
M. Z. White	1914-1918	Warden
J. Z. Terrell	1918-1923	Warden
S. P. Smith	1923-1927	Warden
L. M. Robinson	1927-1929	Warden
A. C. Scroggins	1930-1932	Warden
Dr. C. F. McClintic	1933-1936	Warden
C. M. Stone	1937-1938	Warden
Leo Collinson	1939	Warden
C. M. Stone	1940	Warden
M. E. Ketchum	1941-1946	Warden
Orel J. Skeen	1947-1955	Warden
Ira M. Coiner	1956	Warden
E. H. Tucker	1957	Warden
Donivon E. Adams	1958-1960	Warden
O. C. Boles	1961-1967	Warden
Ira M. Coiner	1968-1971	Warden
Donald E. Bordenkircher	1972-1973	Warden
Arthur McKenzie	1974-1975	Deputy Warden
Arthur L. McKenzie	1976	Warden
Bobby Leverette	1977-1978	Warden
Richard G. Mohn	1979	Warden
Donald E. Bordenkircher	1980-1983	Warden
Manfred G. Holland	1983-1985	Warden
Jerry C. Hedrick	1985-1988	Warden
Carl Legursky	1989-1992	Warden
George Trent	1992-1995	Warden
Paul Kirby	1992-1995	Deputy Warden

But the one who fought the hardest to keep out the electric chair, aptly nicknamed "Old Sparky," was Warden Haddox in 1905. Below is the letter he composed and sent in protest regarding bringing the electric chair to Moundsville.

Letter from West Virginia Penitentiary's Warden to House of Delegates

EDITOR'S NOTE: The following letter was printed in the Journal of the House of Delegates, 1905. (Charleston: Moses W. Donnally, 1905), 291-92. It is reprinted here as an interesting companion to the foregoing article on executions in West Virginia.

West Virginia Penitentiary, Warden's Office
Moundsville, W. Va. Jan. 23, 1905.
To The Members of the House of Delegates:

Late Saturday afternoon while in Charleston I learned for the first time that a bill had been introduced in the House of Delegates abolishing executions by hanging and substituting therefore, electrocution or execution by the electric chair. Subsequent inquiry revealed that this bill was reviewed by the committee on humane institutions and public buildings (instead of the Penitentiary Committee, to which it surely belonged) and that the committee had recommended passage of the bill. I was compelled to leave town early the next day and accordingly address you this letter.

This bill effects materially the official force of this institution, and we view its possible passage with grave concern. Let me say that no greater mistake could be made than the passage of this bill, from the standpoint of humanity, efficiency, safety and economy.

No doubt, the gentleman who prepared and offered this bill was actuated by a feeling of humanity and desired to do what he considered would be a great improvement, with less pain, and less distress, but the very opposite of this is the case.

The present system of conducting executions here is by all means the most humane, the safest and least painful and is less expense [sic]. From the time the subject is started from his cell until he reaches the scaffold, steps on the trap, is bound, strapped, the noose adjusted, the black cap placed, the brief prayer said, and the subject dropped and dead, is less than sixty seconds.

There have been twelve executions here since the law requiring executions at the penitentiary passed, three under my predecessors--nine under my administration. In every case there has not been the slightest hitch or error, and the subject has been subjected to no delay, so terribly hard to stand. Our people know exactly how to do this work and it is done quickly.

But the electric chair is the very opposite. It takes ten minutes to adjust the electrodes (which seems like ten hours), the sponges, and arrange for everything, for everything has to be done with the most absolute precision, and in the only two states that have this system, there have been recently the most unsatisfactory results, and the current has had to be applied over and over, to the great horror and disgust of the officials.

That is not all. Electrocution is the most horrible death known. Every nerve is shattered, every blood vessel *bursted, the bones crushed and broken, and in ten minutes after, every particle of the victim's body is black and blue, a most gruesome sight--exactly what occurs to parts of the victim of a stroke of lightning.*

To maintain an electric chair would involve a large expense, where as the present system involves no expense whatever.

In Ohio and New York they employ an expert electrician at a salary of $1,200.00 per year, who does nothing else but look after the necessary electrical machinery for this purpose alone.

The voltage of the electric current of our dynamos is not sufficient to use for this purpose, at all. We would be forced to purchase a powerful transformer, at a great expense.

The electric chairs are made by only one concern on earth, and cost a fabulous price. The installation of the equipment would cost at least $2,500.00 and the expert would cost $1,200.00 a year, all of which is saved under the present system and is far superior.(1)

I regret very much to have to annoy you with the discussion of the details of a painful subject, but it seems necessary for you to know the facts in this matter.

Previous to having an execution here under my administration, I supposed, like the author of the bill, that electrocutions were more humane and better. But after hearing from their own lips the experiences of the Warden of the Ohio Penitentiary and the Superintendent of Prisons in New York, both of whom denounce their system, and after my subsequent experiences here, I am unalterably opposed to the electric chair. We use electricity to spring the trap, and that it [sic] all the need we have for electricity.

I desire to urge you in the most earnest manner of which I am capable, to vote against this bill, in the interest of humanity, propriety and economy. Our officers are quick to ask for improvements here and had this been regarded as an improvement, we should ourselves have asked for it long since.

I shall thank you to make as much of these views public as in your opinion is necessary and advisable.

Yours truly,

C. E. Haddox,

Warden

The penitentiary's entire power plant was replaced in 1905 at a cost of $9,500, "the expenditure of which is fully justified by the improved conditions, the greatly enhanced efficiency, the economy of operation and the certainty of results." Biennial Report of the Board of Directors of the West Virginia Penitentiary, 1905-1906 (Charleston: Tribune Printing, 1906).

Even with the warden's protests, the electric chair was brought in and the hangings stopped. The electric chair was aptly nicknamed "*Old Sparky*" by the guards at the prison because of the sparks that would fly off of it as it was in use. It was said that, as "*Old Sparky*" took the life of the man who sat within it, the lights throughout the entire prison would flicker then the stench of burnt flesh would be smelled down the hall. At least nine men lost their lives to the electric chair the year it was in use.

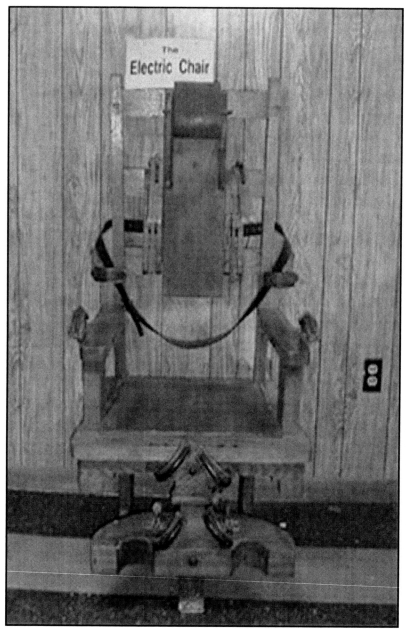

Figure 114. Image of "Old Sparky."

America's Most Proclaimed Haunted Places

But, perhaps the most famous of all the stories associated with Moundsville has to be the story of the "sugar shack." The "sugar shack" was a room in the basement of the prison. This area was used as an indoor recreational area for the prisoners when the harsh winters would come. The sugar shack was known as one of the most violent places within the prison. There were numerous stabbing and rapes that took place within the sugar shack. Oftentimes, a fight would break out in the confines of the sugar shack, leading to many stabbings. One of the myths is that one of the prisoners was attacked and killed in the sugar shack. After countless hours of research and talking extensively to the owner, I have come to determine there was never an actual, documented death in the sugar-shack. Even though, most who have visited the old prison state it is the sugar-shack where they feel the most uncomfortable. This, in my opinion, is due to the basement being the darkest place within the prison. Often when one finds themselves in a dark, enclosed space, a feeling of hopelessness will overcome them. Not necessarily due to a haunting, but more due to the human mindset and customs.

Many class A EVPs have come out of the old prison, along with reports of many sightings of a shadow man who will oftentimes follow one around within the death hall area. There have been claims made by the people taking the tour of the old prison of having been touched, and in some cases, of even being shoved. This old prison has indeed been claimed as one of the most well known paranormal "hot spots" in the country. For anyone interested in the paranormal world, or even the historical aspects of corroborating history with actual recorded evidence, Moundsville will never let them down.

Moundsville is one of my favorite places I had the honor of putting within this book. The people who run the old prison now, are the type of people that always make you feel at home. This is one of the places I will tell everyone I know they should definitely visit. This place is very active. If you are not a believer when you first enter the building by the time you leave this old prison you will be.

One more point worth mentioning; it is a well know fact that, at one time, Charles Manson sent a letter requesting a transfer to Moundsville. Some stories will lead you to believe he was there, but the truth of the matter is Manson was never incarcerated in Moundsville Penitentiary.

~ CHAPTER TWELVE ~

~ Trans-Allegheny Lunatic Asylum ~
Weston, West Virginia

The History of Trans-Allegheny Lunatic Asylum

Construction started on the Trans-Allegheny Lunatic Asylum in the late 1850's. Mainly constructed by the use of prison labor, the first prisoners to arrive were black men from a nearby prison. However, the construction work was placed on hold in 1861, during the Civil War. The government moved troops in and used the large, partially constructed building for its own purposes. After the admission of West Virginia as a state in the US in 1862, the construction started again. In October of 1864, the first patients were admitted. The completion of the children's ward in 1881 finalized the construction process and made The Trans-Allegheny Lunatic Asylum a fully contained facility.

In most cases, the Asylum encouraged families to stay away; believing it was better for the patients to be completely isolated from them. This often left children alone and frightened. The

157

Figure 115. The asylum as it was in the late 1800's.

Figure 116. The asylum as it sits today.

Figure 117. Photograph found of some of the facility's juvenile patients after it closed.

children's ward was always alive with action and energetic youth, the children running up and down the hallways.

It is documented Doctor Freeman, the same Doctor Freeman from Northern State Hospital mentioned earlier in this book, came to the Trans-Allegheny Lunatic Asylum and performed some of his first "Ice Pick" lobotomies there. For most of Trans–Allegheny's patients, the fourth floor was one that even the mere mention of would send fear rippling through them. It was known as the medical floor. With the Lobotomy fast becoming the cure all for the insane, and Doctor Freeman on staff for this very purpose, he had an endless stream of victims to experiment with. As his work became extremely well known, Doctor Freeman often traveled around to a number of different asylums and performed his signature "Ice Pick Lobotomy."

For most of the patients, the fourth floor stay was almost

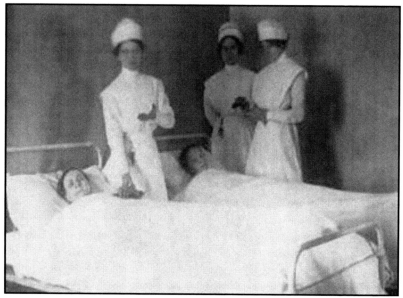

Figure 118. The above photograph shows staff nurses caring for the sick children.

Figure 119. The entry to the Asylum seemed like a welcoming place.

160

Figure 120. A undated photo of the waiting room..

Figure 121. The old wheel chair still sits within the front area.

Figure 122. A view of some of the patient's rooms on the 2nd floor, as they are now.

America's Most Proclaimed Haunted Places

Figure 123. Inside view of a patient's room.

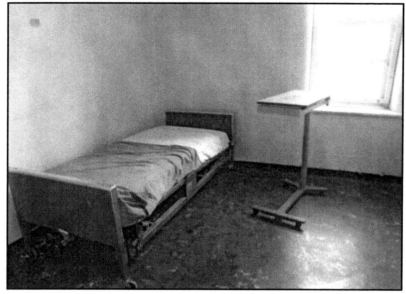

Figure 124. Patient's room with bed.

always a one way trip to the basement and the morgue. With the new surgery being tried all over the country and still in its experimental stage, many were led to believe that electric shock administered until the patient was unconscious coupled with the "Ice Pick" Lobotomy was the only way to cure the insane.

Many so called "treatments" were used at the Trans-Allegheny Lunatic Asylum but the most common ones were as follows:

Water treatment- Patients were submerged in a tub filled with ice water and left in it for extended periods of time. Alternatively, they were also wrapped in sheets soaked in ice water and "rested".

Shock Therapy- Electric shock was administered to the patients while submerged in water tanks. Oftentimes, and more commonly, electric shock was applied directly to the temples by the application of "brain- shock electrodes."

The Lobotomy- Patients had their skulls opened and their nasal

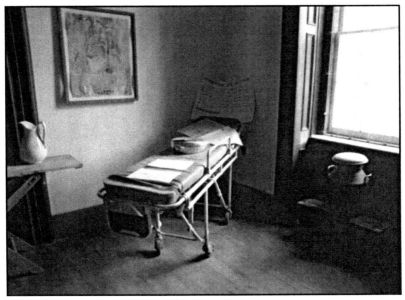

Figure 125. The medical room.

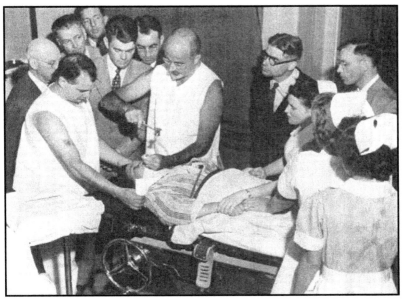

Figure 126. Doctor Freeman teaching the lobotomy at Trans-Allegheny Lunatic Asylum in 1949.

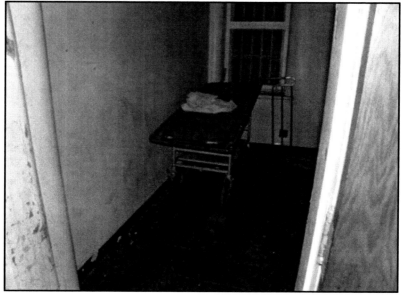

Figure 127. Embalming table in the morgue.

Figure 128. Slab tables still remain within the basement of the old asylum.

passages separated mid way through the brain, in most cases the patients did not live.

Now, Trans-Allegheny Lunatic Asylum was not the original name. The Asylum was known by many names over the many years it was open. Weston State Hospital was one of those names. Regardless of its name, the asylum was known to be the most violent Asylum of the day. It is documented that in the last twenty years of the Asylum's operation, a number of female nurses were violently raped.

In one case, a nurse had been reported missing after she went to the fifth floor for a bed check. As the hours passed, her co-workers began to worry and went to the fifth floor looking for her. When they could not locate her, they called in the police. The Asylum went into lock down, and the police began to search the Asylum, as well as the grounds. It seemed as if she had simply disappeared. Two long months passed. One night, a nurse using the backstairs, which were hardly ever used, came across the missing nurse's body. Once again the police were called out to the Asylum. Today it still remains a mystery of just what happened to the nurse. Her killer was never found.

After digging through days of archives, I was able to find documents to support this claim. A nurse, Amber Shaffer, did go missing two hours into her shift on her second week at the asylum. It was not until ten weeks later her decomposing body was found in a stairwell in the back of the asylum. She was thirty-two years old.

Once the asylum was shut down, the stories really began to come to life, as they often do. And, like most old buildings, the stories of haunting and ghosts traveled to almost every state. One of the stories told at the old asylum is that of a security guard. The security guard had been making his rounds and heard a noise while on the fourth floor. He called out. There was no answer. When he shined his flashlight down the hall, he caught a glimpse of someone walking into a room half-way down the hall. As he called out again, there still was no answer. As he walked to the room, where only a moment earlier he had watched the person walk into the room, he stopped at the door way shining his flashlight into the dark room. He did not see anyone!

As he searched the small room, there was no one inside. Satisfied his eyes were playing tricks on him, he turned to walked out, when something grabbed him! He suddenly found himself being pulled back into the room. Then as he struggled to get free, he once again realized he was alone in the room. After that, he fled the old asylum never to return. He resigned his post that very night. However, there is no documented proof of this whatsoever.

Although, there are similar claims being made by some of the people employed to give tours there now. Many of those claims focus on the same room on the fourth floor. But, with no documentation or evidence to support those claims, it is simply a great story. I must say there is a lot of evidence in the archives to support a lot of deaths within this particular old Asylum. However, we must keep in mind that, like most of the asylums back in the 1900's, tuberculosis was a sure death. If the disease did not kill you back then, the cure most assuredly would. Doctor Freeman was often at this asylum, a well known fact, and as you could see by the info on him in the Northern State section of this book, death seemed to follow him everywhere he went.

~ CHAPTER THIRTEEN ~

~ Murder Ridge ~
Mohawk, Ohio

For most, traveling down a long, dark stretch of road, through the middle of nowhere breathes paranoia and fear into them. But, for the people who live in Ohio, it is more than some ghost story or a movie that brings on this fear; for them it is all too real Just outside of Walhonding, Ohio, is a sleepy little farming town in the northwest corner of Coshocton County. During the 1950's, it was home to a family by the name of Reese.

The Reese family had two children; a girl named Ethel Reese and a son, Cletus Reese. Their son suffered a mental disability and would often fly into unprovoked fits of rage. At almost six foot three, and three hundred pounds, he was well known around the small town as a guy no one wanted to upset. Most of the town residents lived in fear of Cletus. Soon, they would find that fear justified.

In the 1950's, travelers along Route 26 began to disappear. They often broke down along a stretch of dark, desolate road. Then

Figure 129. Home in Castle Township where Cletus Reese lived.

Figure 130. Image of Cletus Reese.

a tow truck would come out of nowhere with seemingly lucky timing and offer to help out. Somewhere between the stretch of road and the small shop behind the family farm, the travelers would disappear. The car would end up being parted out. The disappearance of a Fresno, California, high school teacher who moonlighted part-time as a car salesman, Clyde Patton, caused things to begin unraveling for the Reese family.

Clyde went missing while accompanying a customer on a test drive on Wednesday June 2, 1954. When Clyde failed to return from the test drive, the car lot called the police and made a report. Only a few hours later, the police found the car. When Cletus Reese showed up at his house with the new car, his sister Ethel, knowing something was not right, called the police. Once the police arrived, they discovered it was the same car reported missing along with Clyde Patton. As the police looked around the old farm, they found the body of Clyde Patton, in a shallow, make-shift grave. His head had been completely caved in.

After the body of Clyde Patton was found the police took Cletus and taped off the farm as a crime seine. What they would find confirmed the fear the town had in Cletus Reese.

As the police began to unearth more and more bodies, they cuffed Cletus. Due to his size, it took three pairs of cuffs to detain him.

As night fell on the farm, word spread quickly and the town's residents started to come forward with stories of the Reese family frequently taking in drifters and boarders. People had seen the boarders arrive, but no one could ever remember any of them leaving.

The second murder victim was believed to be Lester Melick , missing since November 28th. Cletus admitted to the murders, but claimed the voice of Mrs. Truman told him to do it. Mrs. Truman

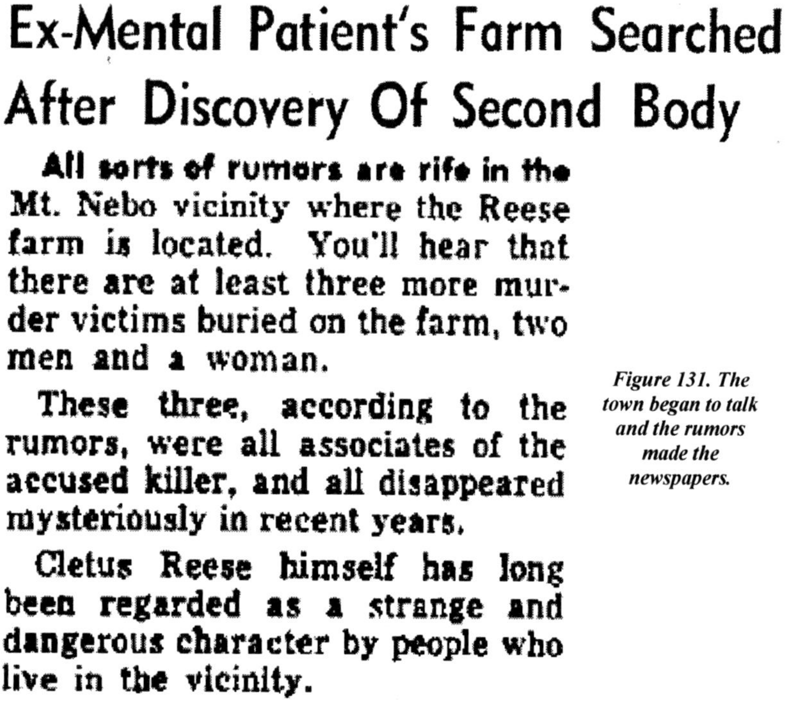

Ex-Mental Patient's Farm Searched After Discovery Of Second Body

All sorts of rumors are rife in the Mt. Nebo vicinity where the Reese farm is located. You'll hear that there are at least three more murder victims buried on the farm, two men and a woman.

These three, according to the rumors, were all associates of the accused killer, and all disappeared mysteriously in recent years.

Cletus Reese himself has long been regarded as a strange and dangerous character by people who live in the vicinity.

Figure 131. The town began to talk and the rumors made the newspapers.

was one of the voices that had long been talking to him, telling him to do things. Mrs. Truman was the same voice he claimed to hear while he was in Cambridge State Hospital where he was diagnosed as a paranoid schizophrenic with homicidal tendencies. It was there he met one of his first victims, a man named Paul Tish, aged thirty-nine. The last time Tish was seen occurred a few days after Cletus was sent home to his family. Paul escaped from Cambridge Hospital on December 8, 1952, and was seen walking up the drive to the Reese farm.

The Cambridge State Hospital was well known for the brutal abuse of patients. In the children's ward, they often kept the children in cages. For the adults, it was far worse.

The old hospital was closed down and now sits abandoned. With Cletus's past history of being in the state hospital, he never

172

Third Body Found On Reese Farm

BELIEVED TO BE THAT OF MISSING DANVILLE MAN

The body of a third man, believed to be that of Lester Melick, 58, missing from his Danville home since Thanksgiving, was found on the Cletus Reese farm near Nellie at about 1:30 p. m. today.

A large searching party headed by Gilbert Kempf, Coshocton, and Paul Cochran, Knox county, was reported to have found the body. Mr. Melick had two dental plates and so did the body of the man found today.

Over 50 men were searching over the 200-acre farm in a thorough manner after the body of an unidentified man was found in a shallow grave behind the Reese home Thursday evening.

The remains of a second man were discovered late Thursday afternoon on the farm of Cletus Reese in the Nellie vicinity, not far from where the body of Clyde Patton, 28, West Lafayette, was found last Saturday morning.

Coshocton county Sheriff Gilbert Kempf stated that two men, Harry Melick, Centerburg, a son of Lester Melick, missing from Danville since Thanksgiving, and Dudley Woolson, Mt. Vernon Route 2, discovered the remains shortly before 4 p. m.

The men notified Knox county Sheriff Paul Cochran and Sheriff Kempf, who went immediately to the scene. In a shallow grave about 100 yards behind the farm home the officials uncovered the remains of a man believed to have been buried for at least a year.

The two men had been searching the farm for several hours when they saw the patch of disturbed ground and several bits of cloth in the vicinity which led them to believe it might be a grave.

Sheriff Kempf stated that the body was not that of Melick, who has been missing since last Thanksgiving. The body in the shallow grave was that of a fairly heavy man, and had been clothed in a brown leather jacket and brown oxford type shoes, size 9 or 9½ and of the moccasin toe type. The man had worn a 38-inch belt.

The skull revealed a large fracture on one side, and a piece had been broken off. The body, which was in advanced state of decomposition, was taken to the Glass funeral home in Coshocton for further disposition.

Sheriff Kempf stated this morning that there was no clue to the identity of the man found Thursday. Reese was taken along to the scene yesterday but would not comment when questioned. He just stood by the grave and stared.

Dudley Woolson, Mt. Vernon Route 2 (left) and Harry Melick, Centerburg mortician, son-in-law of missing Lester Melick of Danville, who found remains of unidentified man in shallow grave on Reese farm.

Figure 132. Undated newspaper showing headlines of discovered bodies.

spent one day in prison for his crimes. Instead, he was handed over to the maximum security ward of Lima State Hospital. This was a far better place than he deserved and was far better than the Cambridge State Hospital he had been in. The Lima State Hospital was no stranger to people like Cletus Reese, soon Cletus found himself right at home in the hospital.

It was at the Lima State Hospital Cletus P. Reese spent the rest of his life. Cletus died on May 15, 1966, and was buried at the

Figure 133. Newspaper photo of sheriff and deputy examining the remains in a shallow grave.

Darling Run Cemetery in Jefferson Township.

It would seem the death of Cletus P. Reese would bring the end of the story, but that is certainly not the case. Route 26 became known as "Murder Ridge," and for good reason. Today, the old Reese farm still stands, dark and desolate, as it had so long ago. The bodies of all the victims still have not to this day been found. There may be more, lying somewhere within the grounds of the old Reese farm. To this day, no one knows just how many victims there really were. I talked to the Coshocton County Sheriff's Department to try and find out the truth of what actually took place at the old Reese

Figure 134. The old hospital as it sits today.

Figure 135. Old photo of the children's ward in Cambridge State Hospital.

175

Figure 136. Lima State Hospital only days after it opened.

Figures 137 & 138. Grave marker and obituary for Cletus Reese.

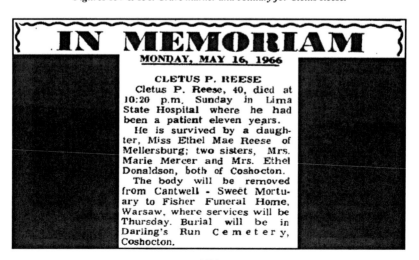

IN MEMORIAM

MONDAY, MAY 16, 1966

CLETUS P. REESE

Cletus P. Reese, 40, died at 10:20 p.m. Sunday in Lima State Hospital where he had been a patient eleven years.

He is survived by a daughter, Miss Ethel Mae Reese of Mellersburg; two sisters, Mrs. Marie Mercer and Mrs. Ethel Donaldson, both of Coshocton.

The body will be removed from Cantwell - Sweet Mortuary to Fisher Funeral Home, Warsaw, where services will be Thursday. Burial will be in Darling's Run Cemetery, Coshocton.

farm. I was unable to get any information.

After having no luck with the local authorities, I decided to try my luck with the neighbors and residents from nearby at the time of the murders. I eventually tracked down and got in touch with one of the people who lived on a farm near the Reese farm at the time of the murders. I interviewed a woman named Ellyn. She recalls going to the Reese farm with her father when she was about eight years old. It was at this time I got a much better, insightful, first hand account into the way the Reese family truly was.

Cletus lived in the farm house with his sister, after their mom and dad passed away. The town knew Cletus as the type of guy who was always willing to lend a helping hand. He was a quiet guy. The family kept to themselves, mostly. Cletus' sister was afraid of her brother, Ellyn recalled. Cletus would often bring home people for dinner. Ethel would cook for them, not knowing the dinner she made would be their last meal. Ellyn recalled hearing the stories that spread through the town. She especially remembers the stories of Ethel and how she came to find out who Cletus really was and what her brother was doing.

One night, the night when her brother came home with the new car, Ethel knew something was wrong. She made dinner and claimed not to have any butter. She told her brother she was going to the next farm over to borrow some. Once in the safety of the other house, she had them call the sheriff. Ethel then waited until Sherriff Keppf arrived. At that time the body of the salesman was found. With full knowledge of Cletus' past, they put him in a straight jacket. Cletus asked them to take it off him. When they did not, he ripped out of it.

At that time, Ellyn told me, he fed the murder victims to their hogs they raised and bred to sell or use for food. What the hogs did not eat, "he would place in the field", she said. While he was at the police department, he allegedly told the police that, "if anyone moved in to his house he would kill them". For a long time, no one would move into the old Reese farm house for fear Cletus would break out of jail and kill them.

Many of the town's people today, still believe the spirits of the murder victims wander the Reese's land. On several occasions, the police have been called out to the old farm to investigate sightings of a large man walking around the house late at night. Always, when the police arrive, there is no one around. I have called the sheriffs' department and they indeed confirmed this claim. The old Reese farm remains steeped in mystery to this day. The victims, the ghosts, and indeed Cletus, himself, are enticing us to further investigate. Perhaps one day, the whole truth will be brought to light. And the restless souls of the Reese farm will be allowed to rest in peace.

~ CHAPTER FOURTEEN ~

~ The Pride House ~
Jefferson, Texas

Anyone who has stayed overnight within the Pride house knows one thing; even when one is alone in the room, they are never really alone. It has oft been reported that as one sits alone in their room, they feel as though something is watching their every move. Sometimes, late at night, when all within the house is quiet, guests will lie awake in their beds and hear her. It seems Jenny has never really left the house, even after her death. Paranormal teams from all over come to the Pride House to get just one good piece of evidence. The Pride house always gives it to them. I must say, as I would talk to Jenny, the current owner of the Pride house, I would often hear a man's voice in the background. Yet, no man lives there...

This house was once known as the Brown House and was built in 1889. As old as it is, there are records on the land stating there was another house on the same land prior to the house there now. I came across some notes regarding the death of a small boy named

Figure 139. Recent photo of the Pride house.

William T Brown—a five year old boy who drowned. Now, whether or not this boy lived in the previous house or the current house is unclear. However, many of the paranormal teams who stayed overnight at the Pride House, often caught EVP's of a small child. The spirits of the Pride House seem to want to interact with the people who come to visit. I have spent months looking for records on the Pride House; everything and anything from birth to death, etc.

It seems the only truth to be found is the truth uncovered within the evidence caught by those who have come to this beautiful place. The rest is lost with its past. This, sadly, is because most of the historical documents were either buried and hidden so deeply they cannot be found, or, as is common with places this old, the historical documents have been destroyed. While I genuinely continue to seek this historical accounting, the substantial amount

Figure 140. Undated photo of the Brown family members on a warm summer day.

of evidence collected from investigations there cannot be ignored.

This one broke my heart. It is one of the greatest places there is. So much has been collected, it simply cannot be ignored due to lack of historical documentation. And what I have been able to dig up, does correlate with the evidence gathered. So, I will include what I do know is truth then let our readers judge the Pride House for themselves.

The house was built by a family, the Browns, who were well known in town as one of the more prominent families. In 1901, tragedy struck heavily on the Brown family. On December 25, 1900, as the crisp December air fell on Christmas morning, the fire warmed the living room of their home. The oldest daughter, a lovely young lady with long blond hair, stood by the fireplace with her back turned to the fire, opening her presents. A draft came down the chimney and caught the back of her dress on fire. As

Jenny ran from the house to the out side, one of the maids followed her, and helped to put her out on the front yard. Jenny suffered from third degree burns over sixty percent of her body. Jenny's father carried her back into the house and lay her on her bed, immediately sending someone to summon the town doctor. Thirty-three days later, on January 28,1901, Jenny Brown died from the burns she sustained on that fateful Christmas morning. Her time of death was three a.m. I have tried to find the death records on Jenny but have been unable to do so. But there was an article in the obituaries to support the story of Jenny's death. Her mother, unable to truly cope with the sudden and tragic loss of her daughter, slipped into a deep state of depression. She died of a broken heart.

The house changed hands a few times before becoming known as the Pride House. But according to the research, the Brown/Pride House was not the only house to ever sit in that exact spot on the land. There had been another house. Curiously enough the prior house also caught fire on Christmas Day, but in 1836, and burned to the ground. There are no death records on file for that fire. After the fire, the present day Pride House, currently sitting on the land was built. The fire which took Jenny's life occurred sixty-four years to the day after the first fire.

Now for me, this would have been just one of those weird coincidences to blow off, if I had not come across mention of yet another fire... One which took the life of the owner on Christmas Day in1965, exactly 64 years since the last fire and the death of Jenny. To this date, the Pride House has become one of Texas' most loved bed and breakfasts. Today, paranormal teams come from all over the country to find the evidence they continually seek. The Pride House always delivers.

Out of all the places I have ever been, the most class A Evp's ever caught at one time have come from the Pride House. For anyone who wants to step back in time, with all the comforts of home, while enjoying some great food along with a down-home feeling, the Pride House cannot be beat. And for any of the paranormal teams looking for your next great research spot, this is one place you need to go. It is a place that, as we were putting this book together, we felt like including so readers can go have the house tell the history itself. This place can be booked for any day, whether booking the entire place or just one room. The Pride house is the type of place to leave you wanting more. The owner, Jenny, is a down-to-earth woman who makes certain her guests are taken car of. Out of any of the places I included in this book and to all paranormal investigators; this is the one place that is a must to visit.

~ CHAPTER FIFTEEN ~

~ Myrtles Plantation ~
St. Francesville, Louisiana

The History Behind Myrtles Plantation

The old plantation was built in 1794, by a man named General David Bedford. David lived there alone until 1799 when he sent for his wife and five children to come from Pennsylvania. After David's death, his daughter, Sara, and her husband James Woodruff, moved in with her recently widowed mother, Elizabeth, and managed the plantation.

Sara and James had three children of their own. In 1823, Sara died of yellow fever leaving James and her mother to care for the three children. Only a year later, James died of the yellow fever, as well. Elizabeth was left on her own to take care of the children. Clark, her youngest daughter's husband, moved in to help manage the plantation and help with the children. In 1830, Elizabeth passed away and Clark remained on the property, until three years later. He then sold the plantation, the land, and the slaves to Ruffin Gray.

184

Figure 141. The house as it may have appeared when David Bradford lived in it in 1794. Within the photo is a slave known to be the one legend claims to be Chloe.

Figure 142. The plantation as it sits today.

Figure 143. Portrait of General David Bedford.

Ruffin Gray lived in the house for seventeen years, until his death in1851.

After the death of her father, Gray's daughter took over the plantation alongside her husband. Stirling and Mary began an extensive renovation and remodeling of the old plantation. Once completed, the house was twice the size it once was and it was renamed "The Myrtles." Mary had nine children, but five of them died of yellow fever, leaving her with four surviving children. Stirling died a short time later in 1858.

Mary then hired her son-in-law, William Drew Winter. William and Sara had six children. In the summer of 1871, William was confronted by a man who shot him on the porch of the grand plantation. As William stumbled through the front door of his house, he made it to the top of the steps before collapsing in his wife's arms. This is documented by a death certificate.

After his death, Mary remained on the plantation until her death in 1880, leaving the plantation to her son Stephen. With the plantation in deep debt, Stephen was forced to sell it in 1886. Between 1886 and 1891, the plantation changed hands again. A gaping hole was left within the vital records of the land until a man by the name of Harrison bought it. Over the next few decades, the land was split amongst the Harrison family members. In 1950, the plantation house was sold to Marjorie Munson. The new owner noticed weird things taking place within the house; voices whispering when no one else was there, things moving by themselves, doors opening and closing on their own, etc.

The owner decided to talk to the neighbors about the history of the house and, at that time, the stories of murder came into play. The plantation changed hands a few more times before it was bought by those who are still the owners today. The present owners have the same claims Marjorie once did. The new owners openly seek information about their haunting and the spirits residing within the old plantation house.

The Legend of Myrtles Plantation

One of the most talked about legends is that of a slave named Chloe. Rumor has it, she was forced to be a sex slave for her master named Woodruff. Allegedly, she had been eavesdropping outside his door, and having been warned about eavesdropping before, he cut off her ear. As legend would have it, Chloe would get her revenge on his birthday. It has been said that Chloe placed Oleander leaves in the cake, which are toxic and can cause death when ingested. But alas, it was her master's wife, Sara, and their two children who would eat the cake. Legend says Sara and the two children died of the misplaced poisoning attempt. And for Chloe, her punishment was to be hung from the tree out in front of the house.

America's Most Proclaimed Haunted Places

Historical documents tell us Sara and one of her daughters, Cornelia, died of yellow fever and the other child, Mary, lived a long and healthy life, subsequently having several children of her own. The records also show the Woodruffs never owned any slaves. I have looked into this, extensively, and have found no record of a slave named Chloe or any record of slaves at all.

This photo was taken in broad daylight. There was no one around at the time. I have spent years researching this and looking up that, trusting the history I find is truth. But I must say this photo has me second guessing myself. I had a friend of mine take a look at this photo to see if there was any way it may have been altered. In his expert opinion, this photo has in no way been tampered with. Could it be that the history could have been wrong? I dug a little deeper and came to find that when a slave was sold with the property, the new owner did not always claim them on paper, leaving loopholes and possible windows of opportunity for Chloe to sneak in. This could account for the absence of slave ownership in the Woodruff Historical Property Documents. It is on record that their parents owned slaves.

The next legend is that of a young girl with blond hair walking the upstairs floors late at night. Now, it is documented that several children died within the house, succumbing to yellow fever. However, there have been no photos found to support this.

The third legend is of an Indian woman wandering the grounds outside the house. It is said the old plantation was built on a burial ground. This I can debunk, as I personally looked into the land deeds, and the plot in question was never an Indian Burial Ground. As a matter of fact, the only verified deaths in the house are those of: seven children who passed away from yellow fever, Sara and her husband, James, who also died of yellow fever, and David and Elizabeth who died of old age within the house, as well as Willian's

Figures 144 & 145. This photo above (close-up below) is one of the most famous ones used as evidence for calling the old plantation haunted

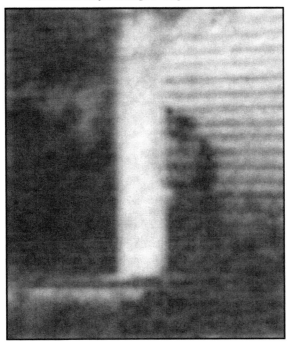

death by gunshot wound. There are twelve documented deaths that can be proven to have taken place within the old plantation house

But, like a lot of old plantations back then, many families were born, lived, and died within their own homes without public records being kept. Yellow Fever- is transmitted through the bite of the female mosquito. It was introduced to America through the slave trade in the 16th century. Yellow Fever causes a high fever with nausea and is accompanied by pain throughout the body. After several days, the body enters a toxic phase, which causes liver damage and eventually death. It was not uncommon back in the 17 and 1800's for yellow fever to, in some cases, take out an entire family. It was, at the time, one of the leading causes of death.

Last but not least, let's not forget William who was shot on his own porch. Even though, no one was ever found to be the killer, some state it was an argument brought on over land. Most of the deceased are buried close by the old plantation. It was stated that Lewis died in 1854, but you can see by the records below, that he indeed passed away in 1858.

Stirling (Lewis and Family) Papers 1784-1938
Biographical/Historical Notes

Lewis Stirling (1786-1858) was the son of Alexander (d.1808) and Ann Alston Stirling. On July 14, 1807, Lewis wed Sarah Turnbull (d.1875); they resided at Wakefield Plantation in West Feliciana Parish. Stirling owned three additional plantations in Louisiana: Arboreta (West Baton Rouge Parish), Solitude, and Attakapas (St. Mary Parish). Cotton and sugar were cultivated on these plantations, although cotton was the more prevalent crop prior to 1850. The Stirlings also owned a house on waterfront property in Pascagoula, Mississippi. Stirling served as a lieutenant in the 10th

Regiment of the Louisiana Militia during the War of 1812. He received a commission as quartermaster of that regiment from Governor William C.C. Claiborne in 1814, at which time Stirling provided supplies for the Louisiana troops.

The Stirlings had six children: Catherine, Anne, James, Lewis, Daniel, and Ruffin. James, Lewis, and Daniel were educated at St. Joseph's College in Bardstown, Kentucky. Lewis pursued further studies at Yale University in New Haven, Connecticut. During the Civil War, members of the Stirling family took a number of slaves and moved to Natchitoches, Louisiana, and then Smith County, Texas, where they lived near Canton until the war's end. Stirling's son, Lewis, earned the title of colonel during the Civil War.

As members of Grace Episcopal Church in St. Francisville, Louisiana, the Stirlings donated money for construction of the structure and the family cemetery is located on the church grounds. As we all know, with old houses there are always great stories to be told. Even though there is some activity within the old house, the stories and the documentation do not correlate or match up with the history. Is it haunted? I believe that something haunts the old plantation. As to the identity of the ghosts? Confirming who they claim them to be isn't substantiated by anything historically documented. There is just not enough evidence to support the claims.

America's Most Proclaimed Haunted Places

.

CPSIA information can be obtained at www.ICGtesting.com
Printed in the USA
LVOW091603090812

293690LV00012B/31/P

9 780984 614394